DIGITAL IMAGE AND VIDEO WATERMARKING AND STEGANOGRAPHY

Edited by **Sudhakar Ramakrishnan**

Digital Image and Video Watermarking and Steganography
http://dx.doi.org/10.5772/intechopen.75155
Edited by Sudhakar Ramakrishnan

Contributors

Srinivas Bachu, Aravind Kumar M, Pranab Kumar Dhar, Raqib Hasan, Tetsuya Shimamura, Krishna Bhowal, Maha Bellaaj, Kais Ouni, Sudhakar Ramakrishnan

Notice

Statements and opinions expressed in the chapters are these of the individual contributors and not necessarily those of the editors or publisher. No responsibility is accepted for the accuracy of information contained in the published chapters. The publisher assumes no responsibility for any damage or injury to persons or property arising out of the use of any materials, instructions, methods or ideas contained in the book.

First published in London, United Kingdom, 2019 by IntechOpen
IntechOpen is the global imprint of INTECHOPEN LIMITED, registered in England and Wales, registration number: 11086078, The Shard, 25th floor, 32 London Bridge Street
London, SE19SG – United Kingdom
Printed in Croatia

British Library Cataloguing-in-Publication Data
A catalogue record for this book is available from the British Library

Additional hard and PDF copies can be obtained from orders@intechopen.com

Digital Image and Video Watermarking and Steganography, Edited by Sudhakar Ramakrishnan
p. cm.
Print ISBN 978-1-78984-167-1
Online ISBN 978-1-78984-168-8
eBook (PDF) ISBN 978-1-83962-192-5

We are IntechOpen,
the world's leading publisher of
Open Access books
Built by scientists, for scientists

4,300+
Open access books available

116,000+
International authors and editors

125M+
Downloads

Our authors are among the

151
Countries delivered to

Top 1%
most cited scientists

12.2%
Contributors from top 500 universities

CLARIVATE ANALYTICS
BOOK
CITATION
INDEX
INDEXED

WEB OF SCIENCE™

Selection of our books indexed in the Book Citation Index
in Web of Science™ Core Collection (BKCI)

Interested in publishing with us?
Contact book.department@intechopen.com

Numbers displayed above are based on latest data collected.
For more information visit www.intechopen.com

Meet the editor

Dr. S. Ramakrishnan has 19 years of teaching experience and 1 year of industry experience. He is a professor and Head of the Department of Information Technology, Dr. Mahalingam College of Engineering and Technology, Pollachi, India. He is an associate editor for IEEE Access and a reviewer of 25 international journals, including seven IEEE transactions, five Elsevier science journals, three IET journals, ACM computing reviews, Springer journals, Wiley journals, etc. He is on the editorial board of seven international journals. He is a guest editor of special issues of three international journals, including *Telecommunication Systems Journal* for Springer. He has published 169 papers in international and national journals and conference proceedings. Dr. Ramakrishnan has published two books for CRC Press, USA, each one on cryptography and wireless sensor networks, six books on speech processing, pattern recognition, and fuzzy logic for IntechOpen Publisher, UK, and one book on computational techniques for Lambert Academic Publishing, Germany.

Contents

Preface IX

Section 1   **Introduction   1**

Chapter 1   **Introductory Chapter: Digital Image and Video Watermarking and Steganography   3**
Srinivasan Ramakrishnan

Section 2   **Watermarking   7**

Chapter 2   **Watermarking Technique for Multimedia Documents in the Frequency Domain   9**
Maha Bellaaj and Kaïs Ouni

Chapter 3   **Color Image Watermarking Based on Radon Transform and Jordan Decomposition   31**
Pranab Kumar Dhar, Rakib Hasan and Tetsuya Shimamura

Section 3   **Steganography   47**

Chapter 4   **Detection of Motion Vector-Based Video Steganography by Adding or Subtracting One Motion Vector Value   49**
Srinivas Bachu and Aravind Kumar Madam

Chapter 5   **Multilevel Steganography to Improve Secret Communication   63**
Krishna Bhowal

Preface

Authenticating data such as image, video, and audio is an important task in digital communication. Another critical task is establishing ownership of the copyright. Digital watermarking is a technique used to provide authentication and ownership of the copyright to the data. Too much digitalization of data in the form of image, video, and audio communicated through various web and mobile applications makes authentication a challenging task. Steganography, the art of hiding tiny pieces of data in image, video and audio, can also help in copyright protection, authentication, and access control. This book has four interesting chapters: two chapters on watermarking and two chapters on steganography.

After the Introduction section, the next section of this book is on watermarking and has two chapters. In Chapter 1 of this section, two watermarking techniques for multimedia documents in the frequency domain are presented: one for the audio and another for the image to watermark a video containing two components—audio and image. In Chapter 2, the Radon and Jordan transform-based color image watermarking technique is proposed. This method is robust and provides high-quality watermarked images.

Section 3 is on steganography and also has two chapters. In the first chapter of this section, a motion estimation method for searching the locally optimal motion vector is proposed. In the last chapter, multilevel audio steganography is presented to increase the level of security while transmitting confidential information over public channels or the internet.

Overall this book provides three watermarking and two steganography methods and will be a useful resource for graduate students, researchers, and practicing engineers in the field of electrical engineering.

I would like to express my sincere thanks to all the authors for their contributions and efforts to bring about this wonderful book. My earnest gratitude and appreciation go to IntechOpen Publisher, in particular Ms. Romina Skomersic, Author Service Manager, who has brought together the authors to publish this book. I would like to express my heartfelt thanks to the management, secretary, and principal of my institute. Finally, dearest thanks to my family members and in particular to my cute daughter Abirami.

Dr. S. Ramakrishnan
Professor and Head, Department of Information Technology
Dr. Mahalingam College of Engineering and Technology
Pollachi, India

Introduction

Chapter 1

Introductory Chapter: Digital Image and Video Watermarking and Steganography

Srinivasan Ramakrishnan

Additional information is available at the end of the chapter

http://dx.doi.org/10.5772/intechopen.84984

1. Overview of watermarking and steganography

Watermarking and steganography are important cryptographic operations on images and videos. Watermarking embeds the ownership symbol in images and videos either visually or invisibly. Steganography hides small piece of information in images and videos invisibly. Watermarking is used mainly for copyright protection, whereas steganography is used to send secret messages. **Table 1** presents the difference between watermarking and steganography.

	Watermarking	Steganography
Scope	To provide the ownership	To hide the secret information
Input data	Image or video or multimedia	Any digital data
Secret data	Watermark	Payload
Output data	Watermarked data	Stegodata
Protection	Given to original image	Given to the secret information
Imperceptibility	Required only for invisible watermarking techniques	Highly required
Robustness	Highly required	Desirable
Payload capacity requirement	Moderate	Very high
Challenges	High robustness and good imperceptibility (only for invisible watermark)	Good imperceptibility and high payload capacity

Table 1. Watermarking versus steganography.

2. Applications of watermarking and steganography

Some of the latest applications of the watermarking techniques are (1) copyright protection, (2) digital right management, (3) broadcast monitoring, (4) content integrity, (5) media forensics, (6) fraud and tamper detection, (7) package identification, (8) copy control, (9) user tracking, (10) medical image watermarking, and (11) ownership authentication [1–4].

Similarly, some of the modern use steganography are (1) printer steganography, (2) protection of data alteration, (3) document security, (4) setting of covert channel, (5) distributed steganography, (6) in military, (7) in medical images, (8) online challenge, and (7) corporate espionage [1, 5–8].

3. Challenges in the development of watermarking algorithms

Quality of the watermarking techniques can be accessed through various metrics such as peak signal-to-noise ratio (PSNR), signal-to-noise ratio (SNR), structural similarity index measurement (SSIM), and normalized crosscorrelation (NCC). Most of the real-world application requires good imperceptibility and high robustness. Achieving both of them simultaneously for color images and multimedia documents sought highly efficient watermarking algorithms. Hence, obviously transform domain processing will be the natural choice to meet out these complex requirements.

Fourier transform, discrete cosine transform, radon transform, and wavelet transform are the commonly used transformations for embedding watermarks. Fourier transform provides good resistance against geometric attacks. Discrete cosine transform yields robustness when watermarked images are compressed. Wavelet transform archives good imperceptibility and radon transform can provide good robustness. Though each transform is advantages in its own way, only careful development of watermark embedding and extraction algorithms helps in achieving maximum advantage of the chosen transformation.

Most of these transforms are proving good imperceptibility when some additional decompositions are employed. For example, wavelet transforms and singular value decomposition is the most popular choice. Watermarking techniques should be robust against the following attacks namely (1) cryptographic attacks, (2) removal attacks, (3) protocol attacks, (4) geometric attacks, (5) forgery attacks, (6) low-pass filtering attacks, (7) estimation-based attacks, (8) remodulation attacks, (9) copy attacks, and (10) optimized attacks. Identification of suitable transformation is not only sufficient, but careful development of efficient watermarking algorithms is also required to face these challenges [1–4].

4. Challenges in the development of steganography algorithms

Steganography algorithms can be classified based on the type of data employed as (1) text steganography, (2) image steganography, (3) audio steganography, and (4) video steganography.

Some of the commonly used evaluation criteria are invisibility, payload capacity, robustness against image manipulation attacks, and statistical undetectability. Steganalysis can be used to choose good steganography algorithm. Similar to watermarking techniques, steganography algorithms also require careful design and devolvement in order to withstand the following attacks. (1) visual attacks, (2) statistical attacks, (3) histogram attacks, (4) compression attacks, (5) reformat attacks, (6) structural attacks, and (7) subversion attacks [1, 5–8].

5. Conclusion

In this introductory chapter, applications and challenges of both watermarking and steganography are presented. Researchers continue to develop new and efficient watermarking and steganography algorithms. Since huge amount of data are getting digitized, establishing ownership and sharing them secretly are becoming a challenging task. In this book, five interesting algorithms, three for watermarking and two for steganography, are available.

Author details

Srinivasan Ramakrishnan

Address all correspondence to: ram_f77@yahoo.com

Department of Information Technology, Dr. Mahalingam College of Engineering and Technology, India

References

[1] Ramakrishnan S. Cryptographic and Information Security Approaches for Images and Videos. Florida: CRC Press, Taylor & Francis Group; 2018. ISBN: 9781138563841

[2] Zhao X, Ho AT. An introduction to robust transform based image watermarking techniques. In: Intelligent Multimedia Analysis for Security Applications. Berlin, Heidelberg: Springer; 2010. pp. 337-364

[3] Tiwari A, Sharma M. A Survey of transform domain based semifragile watermarking schemes for image authentication. Journal of The Institution of Engineers (India): Series B. 2012;**93**(3):185-191

[4] Khan A, Siddiqa A, Munib S, Malik SA. A recent survey of reversible watermarking techniques. Information Sciences. 2014;**279**:251-272

[5] Fridrich J. Stegnography in Digital Media Principles, Algorithms and Applications. New York: Cambridge University Press; 2010. ISBN: 9780 521 190100

[6] Cheddad A, Condell J, Curran K, Mc Kevitt P. Digital image steganography: Survey and analysis of current methods. Signal Processing. 2010;**90**(3):727-752

[7] Li B, He J, Huang J, Shi YQ. A survey on image steganography and steganalysis. Journal of Information Hiding and Multimedia Signal Processing. 2011;**2**(2):142-172

[8] Karampidis K, Kavallieratou E, Papadourakis G. A review of image steganalysis techniques for digital forensics. Journal of Information Security and Applications. 2018; **40**:217-235

Watermarking

Chapter 2

Watermarking Technique for Multimedia Documents in the Frequency Domain

Maha Bellaaj and Kaïs Ouni

Additional information is available at the end of the chapter

http://dx.doi.org/10.5772/intechopen.79370

Abstract

In order to secure and maintain the authenticity and integrity of multimedia documents, we use digital watermarking. This discipline can be applied to images, audios, and videos. For this reason, and to be independent of the nature of the signal composing the document to be watermarked, we will propose in this chapter two watermarking techniques, one for the audio and another for the image to watermark a video containing the two components audio and image. MDCT is combined with Watson model and a motion detection algorithm in the image watermarking technique and is combined with a psychoacoustic model to elaborate the audio watermarking technique. For the two techniques, the bits of the mark will be duplicated to increase the capacity of insertion and then inserted into the least significant bit (LSB). We will use an error correction code (Hamming) on the mark for more reliability in the detection phase. To highlight our experimental results point of view robustness and imperceptibility, we will compare the proposed techniques with some other existing techniques.

Keywords: multimedia documents, watermarking, MDCT, Watson model, motion detection, psychoacoustic model, hamming

1. Introduction

The spread of multimedia documents and by virtue of the development of technologies in connection with the computer directs the world toward an era where the digital takes a primordial place. In addition, the development of the Internet and, more generally, the new means of communication authorized the large-scale dissemination of digital data. Despite the mentioned advantages, we are facing serious problems: multimedia documents become unprotected, digital data are distributed in an illegal manner, and copyrights are unprotected.

Where does the digital watermarking come from as a security mechanism complementary to encryption? Its basic idea is to insert the information in a robust and imperceptible way in multimedia documents [1]. On after the literature, digital watermarking has received substantial interest as a research topic in the 90s [2, 3]. For the past 28 years, the work on digital watermarking continue to multiply in order to find watermarking techniques for multimedia documents that must meet the following criteria: robustness against a maximum number of attacks and manipulations, high capacity insertion, and imperceptibility of the mark. An appropriate watermarking system must provide the best compromise between these three main features (**Figure 1**).

A watermarking system is formed mainly by two processes: insertion and detection. A mark W is inserted in a multimedia document M to obtain the watermarked document M' by applying the insertion process. In some watermarking systems, we can use a secret key C to perform the insertion. The marked document M' can undergo transformations, and we obtain the resulting document M''. Subsequently, we move to the detection of the mark. There are several detection schemes which we quote: the private scheme where the original digital document is given to the detector, the mark is detected by comparing the original with the watermarked, and the semi-private scheme which gives an answer in the presence or absence of the mark (true or false) without using the original document and the blind scheme, in which only the secret key is needed to extract the mark. To design a watermarking system, the choice of the insertion area is considered as a very important step [4, 5]. We can distinguish three major fields of insertion: the domain without transformation (spatial domain and time domain), the frequency domain, and the multi-resolution domain. The domain without transformation can be the spatial domain for the image and the video and the time domain for the audio. One of the advantages of the methods operating in this field is that they are very fast, since no initial treatment is necessary. However, such a domain does not offer much resistance against existing attacks. The frequency domain is obtained after the application of a transformation such as fast Fourier transform (FFT), discrete cosine transformation (DCT) [6], etc. The most important benefit of using the transformed domain is that it is already used to prepare multimedia information in communication standards such as JPEG for still images [7], MPEG2 for video sequences [8], and MPEG1 for audio [9]. Techniques operating in the frequency domain have the advantage of being robust against the compression operation, since they use the same space that is used for coding. The development of new compression standards such as JPEG2000 [7] and MPEG4 [8] has led researchers to use other insertion domains as the multiresolution domain [10]. The information represented in this area is well localized in

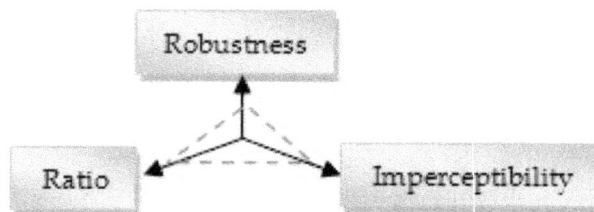

Figure 1. Compromise between robustness, ratio, and imperceptibility.

frequency and time. The sub-band decomposition allows isolating the low frequency components. The middle and high components constitute a less sensitive insertion space.

In the following, we will present some watermarking techniques for video existing in the literature.

- Shaveta and Daljit [11]: in this technique, the authors apply the SWT to the images of the
  video. Subsequently, they apply the SVD to each subband of the red layer. Then, they
  change the singular values of the HH band with the singular values of the HH band of the
  brand. For the other two layers, they select the block with the highest S values and then
  apply the DCT to the selected band. Finally, they insert the mark on each of the selected
  bands. The detection scheme is the inverse of that of insertion.

- Shital et al. [12]: In this article, the author used a watermarking technique to detect
  tampering in a video. The technique operates in the frequency domain using DCT as a
  transformation. After generating the mark (hash value of the frame, the micro-block
  numbers, and the frame number), the latter is inserted into the frames in the frequency
  domain. The insertion is done by replacing the LSB of the highest non-zero DCT coefficient by the bit of the corresponding mark.

- Supriya and Navin [13]: in this chapter, the author proposes a hybrid technique for video
  based on the discrete wavelet transform and singular value decomposition. In this technique, the mark is inserted into the original video images by first converting it into the
  YCbCr color space. Next, the luminance portion (Y component) is broken down into four
  subbands using a discrete wavelet transform. Finally, the singular values of the sub-band
  LL are perceptually shaped by singular values of the image of the watermark. The detection scheme is the inverse of that of insertion.

In this chapter, we will propose a watermarking system for multimedia documents based on
the following ideas:

- The frequency space is a good space points of view robustness and imperceptibility, hence
  the choice of the modified discrete cosine transformation (MDCT) to switch to the frequency domain.

- The temporal methods based on the least significant bit (LSB) provide good results in
  terms of imperceptibility, insertion capacity, and robustness. For these reasons, came the
  idea of using the concept of LSB not in the time domain but in the frequency domain to
  take advantage of the latter.

- To have a blind detection and to reduce the error rate, we had the idea to use a substitute
  method with an error correction code.

- To select the places of insertion, we exploited the properties of the psychoacoustic models
  2 of MPEG 1 for audio component, the properties of the human visual system, the Watson
  model for image component, and a motion detection algorithm to watermarking video.

- Finally, to improve the robustness against attacks, we thought to duplicate the bits of the
  mark several times.

This chapter is organized as follows: in Section 2, we will detail some related works and the process of insertion and detection for the proposed techniques. Section 3 will present the experimental results and compare the results obtained by the proposed watermarking system with other existing in the literature. In the last section, we give a conclusion for this work.

2. The proposed algorithm

2.1. Related works

2.1.1. MDCT

According to the literature, watermarking techniques for still images and videos in the frequency domain use DCT. And since the latter is a block transformation, it can introduce block effects causing noticeable distortions. Then, MDCT has emerged as a very effective and dominant tool in the coding of high quality signals because of its particular properties. The MDCT simultaneously performs critical sampling, reduction of block effects, and flexible windows switching [14]. The coefficients obtained after the application of the MDCT are separated into two bands: high frequencies band and low frequencies band. In our work, we will use a modified version of the MDCT.

The direct and inverse MDCT defined for the audio signal are given by:

$$X(k) = \sqrt{\frac{2}{N}} \sum_{n=0}^{N-1} x(n)\cos\left(\frac{\pi}{N}\left(n+\frac{1}{2}\right)\left(k+\frac{1}{2}\right)\right), \tag{1}$$

where:

- $x(n)$ is the sample number n,
- k is the number of the frequency line ($k \in [0, N-1]$).

$$y(n) = \sum_{k=0}^{N-1} \sqrt{\frac{2}{N}} X(k)\cos\left(\frac{\pi}{N}\left(n+\frac{1}{2}\right)\left(k+\frac{1}{2}\right)\right), \tag{2}$$

where:

- n is the number of the temporal sample, $n \in [0, N]$),
- k is the number of the frequency line $k \in [0, N]$).

For the image, and as we are going to work on blocks of two dimensions, we will use the MDCT for two-dimensional arrays.

The direct and inverse MDCT defined for the image signal are given by:

$$I^{'}(k,l) = \sum_{i=0}^{N1-1} \sum_{j=0}^{N1-1} I(i,j)\cos\left(\frac{\pi}{N1}\left(k+\frac{1}{2}\right)\left(i+\frac{1}{2}\right)\right)\cos\left(\frac{\pi}{N1}\left(l+\frac{1}{2}\right)\left(j+\frac{1}{2}\right)\right), \tag{3}$$

where:

- N1 × N1 size of the image I,

- I(i, j) value of the pixel at position i, j of the image I.

$$J(i,j) = \sum_{k=0}^{N1-1} \sum_{l=0}^{N1-1} I'(k,l)\cos\left(\frac{\pi}{N1}\left(k+\frac{1}{2}\right)\left(i+\frac{1}{2}\right)\right)\cos\left(\frac{\pi}{N1}\left(l+\frac{1}{2}\right)\left(j+\frac{1}{2}\right)\right). \tag{4}$$

2.1.2. Motion detection

To improve the robustness of the video watermarking technique, it is preferable to insert the mark in moving objects [15, 16]. For this reason, we have chosen to use a motion detection algorithm, the one proposed by Peddireddi [17], to identify the objects in motion in the video where we will insert the bits of the mark. The algorithm is composed of four main blocks presented in the following figures (**Figures 2** and **3**).

2.1.3. JND

JND (or just noticeable difference), also known as just perceptible difference or differential threshold, is the minimum amount by which the intensity of the stimulus must be modified to produce a noticeable variation in a sensory experience [18]. This measure is used in the Watson model which consists of the following steps:

- Change the domain of study by calculating the DCT.

- Definition of the quantization matrix. This model uses the Q_m quantization matrix of the JPEG standard [19].

- Calculate the frequencies sensitivity coefficients.

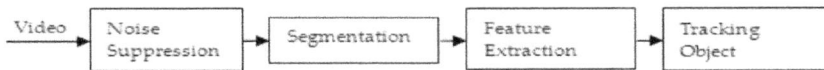

Figure 2. Blocks of the motion detection algorithm.

Figure 3. Detecting the moving object in the video: samplevideo.avi.

- Calculate the sensitivity to the luminance.

- Calculate the contrast masking threshold, M.

- Finally, calculate the quantization error E divided by M to obtain the JND threshold.

$$JND = \frac{E}{M}.$$ (5)

In our work, we will change this model. To achieve the change of the domain study, we will use the MDCT instead of the DCT to exploit its advantages. This choice is also due to the fact that the MDCT has better coding performance than the DCT and also due to the calculation complexity of MDCT which has been reduced in recent years.

2.1.4. Psychoacoustic model

In our work, we will use the psychoacoustic model 2 of the MPEG1 standard. We chose to incorporate this model into our proposed watermarking technique for the audio component of the video, if it exists, in the search for insertion positions. In this model, we do not distinguish between tonal and non-tonal components, but we calculate tonal indices that determine whether the components appear to be tonal or nontonal (noise) [9]. This model is applied on time frames and calculates a masking curve that we will note, *thr ω*.

Figure 4 shows the masking curve *thr ω* for a test signal that has been selected.

2.2. Insertion scheme

The diagram we will adopt can be summarized in **Figure 5**.

In this section, we will give the general principle of the process of inserting the brand for the video watermarking technique. For the realization of this technique, we will adopt a proposed watermarking technique for the still image and another proposed technique for the audio. The insertion is performed at moving objects and in non-successive images. This choice is inspired by the fact that:

- Successive images are strongly correlated, and a mark can be detected and deleted easily by a hacker.

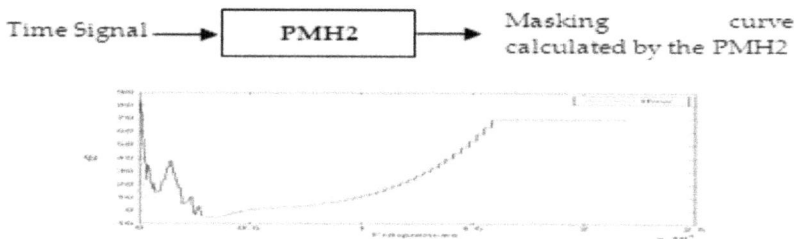

Figure 4. Psychoacoustic model 2, *thr ω*.

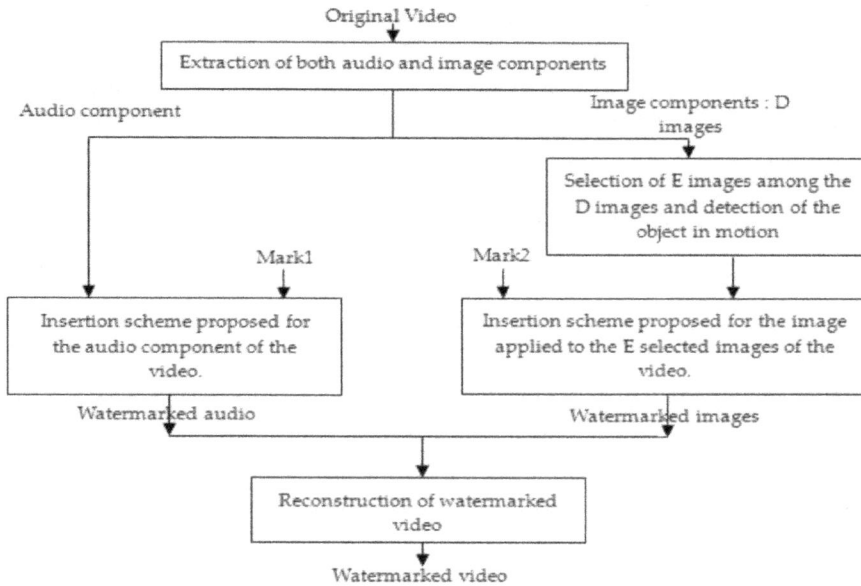

Figure 5. General scheme of insertion of the mark for the video.

- Moving objects are considered a very important factor as, for example, in MPEG4 compression. So, to guarantee a good robustness criterion especially against the compression, we inserted the bits of the mark in the moving objects of the video. We can also improve the invisibility criterion as the mark moves with the objects.

1. The initial input signal is an uncompressed video file. The latter may include or not an audio component.

2. After reading the original video, we proceed to the separation of the two audio and image components. For this reason, the first step is to check if the video has an audio component or not. If the video does not have an audio component, then we extract only the different images constituting the video.

3. In this technique, we will insert the mark "Mark1" in the audio component and the mark "Mark2" in the image component. Before proceeding with the insertion of the two marks, we must binarize them. The insertion process of the proposed technique can integrate any type of mark (text, image, and beep sound). The length of the marks is chosen to be multiple of 8. After binarization of the two marks, we obtain two binary vectors of length multiple of 8. This choice will then be useful for performing a Hamming coding (12,8) [20] on each byte of the binary vectors. The use of the Hamming error correction code makes it possible to improve the detection rate of the two marks, as the inserted bits can be modified (inversion from 0 to 1 or from 1 to 0). It will ensure the correction of errors if necessary. Hamming (12,8) is a linear code whose principle is to add 4 control bits to

encode an 8-bit word. At the end, we obtain two coded bit vectors which represent the two coded marks, of length multiple of 12.

4. To obtain a robust watermarking technique against the different manipulations, we will insert the bits of the mark "Mark2" in no-successive images. Hence, the interest of the module allows to select E images among the D images of the video. Subsequently, we proceed to the detection of the moving object in these images while using a motion detection algorithm. As an output, this algorithm gives the images of the object in motion.

5. Insertion scheme proposed for the image: we will tattoo the different images of the object in motion detected.

    1. Set the block size to (8 × 8) pixels.

    2. Replicate the edges of the image to make its dimensions a multiple of 8.

    3. Decompose the image into blocks of 8 × 8 pixels in the spatial domain.

$$Bloc\_image = \sum_{i=1}^{N1} \sum_{j=1}^{M1} image\_re(i : i + bloksize - 1, j : j + bloksize - 1), \tag{6}$$

    where:

    i = 1...N1 and j = 1...M1 with a step equal to block size = 8.

    4. Move to the frequency domain by applying the MDCT, (Eq. (3)). To obtain the frequency coefficients for each block, we must apply the MDCT for each block of 8 × 8 pixels.

    5. Separate the frequencies and extract the low frequencies band. We chose to insert the mark bits in the low frequencies band as it is much less sensitive to attacks than the high frequencies band. At the end of this step, we obtain for each block all the low frequencies.

    6. Since the human eye is more sensitive to the noise introduced into the low frequency band, we will introduce the Watson model to look for the least perceptible insertion places in the frequencies band. This model calculates the just perceptible difference "JND" for each frequency coefficient of each block.

    7. Substitute the insertion of the mark bits: we will look for insertion positions that belong to the band of low frequencies and allow keeping the mark imperceptible (**Figure 6**).

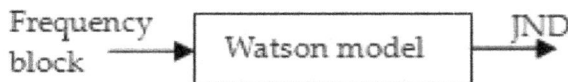

Figure 6. Watson model.

- Select a coefficient of the low frequencies band.

- Binarize the selected coefficient.

- Select the least significant bit (LSB) of the binary representation of the coefficient.

- Substitute the least significant bit by bit stream of watermark to insert.

- Calculate the decimal value of the watermarked coefficient.

- Calculate the difference between the coefficient before the insertion of the mark bit and after the insertion: *Var_coef*.

- Compare this value obtained with that which corresponds to the matrix containing the *JND* values generated by the Watson model.

  - If *Var_coef* < *JND*, so we can insert watermarking bit in this position and we can change the coefficient value without noticing the difference.

  - Else, the insertion in this position will be visible to the eye.

  The insertion is performed on all the blocks of the image to improve the robustness. Therefore, we will proceed with the duplication of bits of the brand *F* times. *F* is calculated according to the number of components where insertion is invisible to the eye, "*NBCom_INV*," and brand size *Lmark*:

  $$F = \frac{NBCom\_INV}{Lmark}. \tag{7}$$

  At the end of this step, we get a watermarked block in the frequency domain.

8. Go back to the space domain by applying the IMDCT (Eq. (4)) to reconstruct the watermarked image.

   All previous steps are applied to all blocks in the image and for all selected images in the video.

6. Insertion scheme proposed for the audio: we will integrate this model in the insertion process to exploit its properties in the search for insertion positions. Similarly, and as for the image, this technique operates in the frequency domain using the MDCT (Eq. (1)). The various steps constituting the insertion process are:

1. Decompose the original audio signal into blocks of 1024 samples each (23 ms duration).

2. Integrate the psychoacoustic model 2 on each time frame of 1024 samples obtained from the previous step. This model will generate a masking curve *thrω*.

3. In parallel with the previous step, apply the MDCT (Eq. (1)) transformation on blocks of 1024 samples to pass to the frequency domain. We obtain blocks of 1024 frequency coefficients in the frequency domain.

4. Extraction of low frequencies: the coefficients obtained are separated at low frequencies and high frequencies. We take each block of frequencies components and set the low frequencies band to half, at the occurrence of N/2 (N = 1024).

5. Substitute insertion: we will inject the watermarking bits into the frequency components of the low frequency band under the masking curve *thrω* (**Figure** 7).

We will look for the insertion positions *Po* belonging to the low frequency band and lying under the curve. After the binarization and the hamming coding of the Mark1, we will obtain a binary sequence *bi* {0, 1} of length Lmark1. In order to improve the robustness criterion of the proposed technique, we duplicated each bit of the sequence *bi*, *F1* times. *F1* is calculated as the integer part of the ratio between the number of components at positions *Po*, *NB_TH* and the length of the mark *Lmark1*.

$$F1 = \text{Integerpart}\left(\frac{NB\_TH}{Lmark1}\right). \tag{8}$$

We will have a binary sequence *b'i* {0, 1} of length *L'mark1*.

$$L'mark1 = Lmark^*F1 \tag{9}$$

After the search for the different frequency components located at the Po positions, we proceed to the binarization of the values of these components. Next, we substitute the least significant bit (LSB) of each component with the current bit of the watermarked message. At the end, we get watermarked block in the frequency domain.

6. Go back to the time domain by applying the IMDCT (Eq. (2)) to reconstruct the watermarked audio. All previous steps are applied to all blocks in the audio.

7. After getting the watermarked audio signal and different watermarked images, we join these two components (audio and image) to form the final watermarked video signal

2.3. Detection scheme

The detection is blind (we do not have the original document; only the secret key is needed to extract the mark) and the reverse of the insertion. For the detection of the two marks Mark1 and Mark2 inserted, we will need as keys *"Key1," "Key2"*:

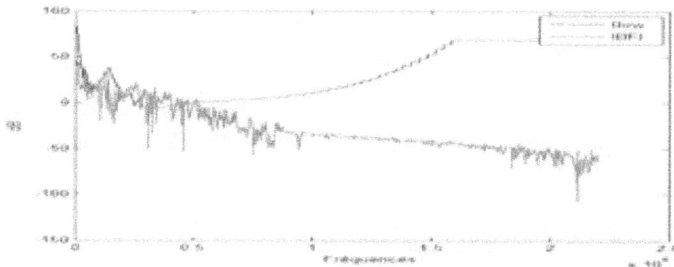

Figure 7. Curve in red "low frequencies" and curve in blue *thrω* for a chosen test signal.

Figure 7 shows the masking curve *thrω* in blue and the curve of low frequencies samples in red for a signal that has been chosen.

- Duplication numbers *F* and *F1* that we can insert a bit.

- List of the positions of the components under the masking curve that are sought by the psychoacoustic model 2 in the insertion phase.

- Positions of the components sought by the Watson model in the insertion phase.

The entry of the detection process is the watermarked video resulting from the insertion process. After separating the two audio components, if it exists, and image and using the two keys (*Key1* and *Key2*), we extract the two marks inserted into each component.

1. Detection scheme proposed for the image: we begin by replicating the edges of the watermarked image, breaking down into blocks size 8×8 pixels in the spatial domain, and applying the MDCT to switch to the frequency domain. Our detection scheme is blind. For this reason, we only use the duplication numbers *F* and the positions of the invisible components generated using the Watson model in the insertion phase.

   1. From these, we can detect the bits of the message inserted in the components correspon-ding to these positions. We will then have as a result a binary vector containing the watermark bits corresponding to the coded signature but with duplication *F* times for each bit. Finally, to detect the bits of the mark without duplication, we use the parameter *F* to eliminate the duplication. We will have as a result the extracted encoded binary brand, of size multiple of 12.

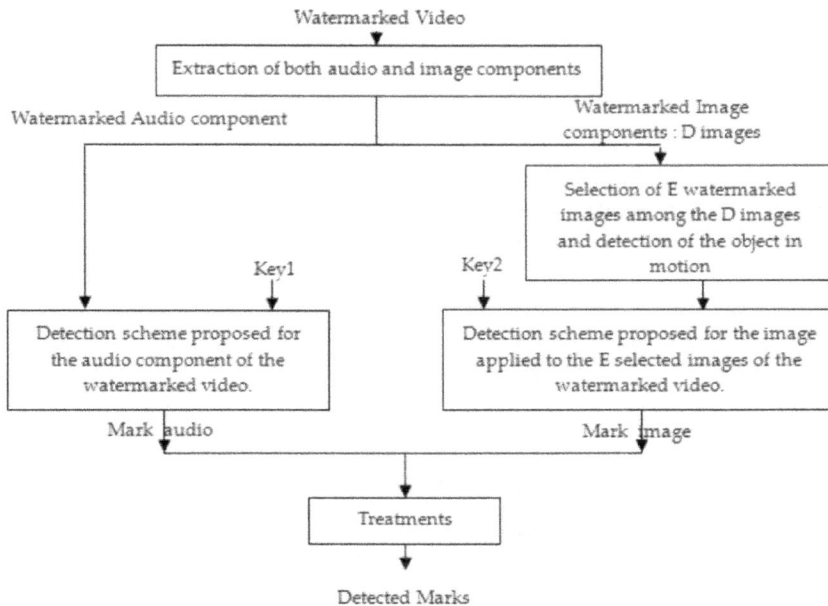

Figure 8. General scheme of detection of the mark for the video.

2. Hamming decoding to finally find useful binary brand, corrected multiple of 8.

3. Reconstruction of the final mark (**Figure 8**).

1. Detection scheme proposed for the audio: after decomposing the watermarked audio signal into blocks of 1024 samples and applying the MDCT on each block to pass to the frequency domain, we proceed to the detection of the bits of the mark.

- From the positions of the watermarked components under the masking curve, sought by the psychoacoustic model 2 in the insertion phase, we determine the values of these components. Subsequently, we proceed, as we did in the insertion process, to the binarization of these values. Then, we extract from the least significant bit of the inserted message. We obtain then a binary sequence with duplication of length *L'mark1*. Finally, to detect the bits of the mark without duplication, we use the parameter *F1* to eliminate the duplication. We will have as a result the extracted encoded binary brand, of size multiple of 12.

- Hamming decoding to finally find useful binary brand, corrected multiple of 8.

- Reconstruction of the final mark.

3. Experimental results and comparative analysis

In this section, we will present, in detail, all the experimental results obtained. The algorithm is tested on MATLAB R2013a with an Intel (R) core (TM) i7-6500U CPU 2.59 GHz, 8 GB memory computer. The experimental corpus is formed by six videos of .avi format (**Table 1**).

3.1. Performance evaluation indexes

3.1.1. PSNR

Peak signal-to-noise ratio (PSNR) is an objective quality evaluation measure whose unit is (dB). It measures the quality of the altered (watermarked) image compared to the original image. In particular, we used the PSNR to evaluate the invisibility of our watermarking system. PSNR is defined as:

$$PSNR_{seq\_video} = 10\log_{10}\left(\frac{255^2}{\frac{1}{RN1M1}\sum_{r=1}^{R}\sum_{n1=1}^{N1}\sum_{m1=1}^{M1}\left(I_{r,n1,m1} - I'_{r,n1,m1}\right)^2}\right), \quad (10)$$

where:

- $I_{r,i,j}$ and $I'_{r,i,j}$: values of pixels (i, j) in the rth image of the original and watermarked video.

- $(M1 \times N1)$: size of the video image.

- R : total number of video frames.

Video (.avi)	Image component	Spectrogram audio component
Windows1		
WildLife11		No audio component
horses		
TV		
Sample		No audio component

Video (.avi)	Image component	Spectrogram audio component
Foreman		No audio component

Table 1. Tested videos.

3.1.2. SNR

Signal-to-noise ratio (SNR) is a measure that will allow us to calculate the similarity between watermarked audio and original audio. It is usually expressed in decibels (dB). SNR is defined as:

$$SNR_{dB} = 10\log_{10}\left[\frac{\left(\sum_n x(n)^2\right)}{\sum_n [x(n) - x'(n)]^2}\right],$$ (11)

where:

- $x(n)$: sample number n of the original signal.

- $x'(n)$: sample number n of the watermarked signal.

3.1.3. Objective difference grade

Objective difference grade (ODG) is a score calculated by the PEAQ algorithm [21]. This algorithm compares the original signal and the watermarked signal and assigns a comparative score between 0 and −4. If ODG = 0, there is no degradation. If we get a GDO rating that varies between −0.1 and −1, the deterioration is noticeable but not annoying. For an ODG rating that ranges between −1.1 and −2, the degradation is slightly annoying. If the ODG value obtained varies between −2.1 and −3, the degradation is annoying. Finally, if the ODG score obtained is in the range [−3, 1; −4] so the distortion is very boring.

3.1.4. Universal quality index

The universal quality index (UQI) is proposed by [22]. It is an objective evaluation of the visual quality of images and whose range of values varies between [0, 1]. Higher UQI values represent a better criterion of imperceptibility. The UQI is defined by:

$$UQI = \frac{4\sigma_{II'}\overline{II'}}{\left(\sigma_I^2 + \sigma_{I'}^2\right)\left[\left(\overline{I}\right)^2 + \left(\overline{I'}\right)^2\right]},$$ (12)

where:

- I and I' are, respectively, the average values of the original image I and the processed image I'.

- σ^2_I and $\sigma^2_{I'}$ are, respectively, the variances of I and I'.

- $\sigma_{II'}$ is the covariance of I and I'.

3.1.5. NC

To test the robustness of the technique against attacks, we will calculate the correlation NC between the original brand inserted and the mark detected after the exposure of watermarked files to different attacks. For the image, the formula for normalized intercorrelation is given by:

$$NC = \frac{\sum_{i,j=1}^{Lmark2} bin(i,j) * bin'(i,j)}{\sqrt{\sum_{i,j=1}^{Lmark2} bin'(i,j)^{2} * \sum_{i,j=1}^{Lmark2} bin(i,j)^{2}}}, \tag{13}$$

where:

- bin is the binary vector of the inserted mark.

- bin' is the binary vector of the mark detected after application of the attacks.

- $Lmark2$ is the length of the inserted mark.

For audio, the formula for normalized intercorrelation is given by:

$$NC = \frac{\sum_{j=1}^{Lmark1} b_i(j) * bin(j)}{\sqrt{\sum_{j=1}^{Lmark1} bin(j)^{2} * \sum_{j=1}^{Lmark1} b_i(j)^{2}}}, \tag{14}$$

where:

- bi is the binary vector of the inserted mark.

- bin is the binary vector of the mark detected after application of the attacks.

- $Lmark1$ is the length of the inserted mark.

3.2. Marks

- *Mark1*: in the audio component of the video, we will insert the text mark "audiowatermarking," of length 136 bits and after the hamming coding, its length reaches 204 bits (after that, each bit will be duplicated $F1$ times).

- *Mark2*: in the image component of the video, we will insert the image "logo.bmp," of size 32×32 pixels and after the hamming coding, its length reaches 1536 bits (after that, each bit will be duplicated F times) (**Figure 9**).

Figure 9. logo.bmp binarised.

Video	PSNR_video	UQI	SNR_audio	ODG
Windows1	62,01	1	63,35	0
WildLife11	59,62	0,99	—	—
Horses	62,28	1	68,52	0
TV	60,78	0,99	62,94	−0.1
Sample	60,4	0,99	—	—
Foreman	53,9	0,99	—	—

Table 2. Experimental results.

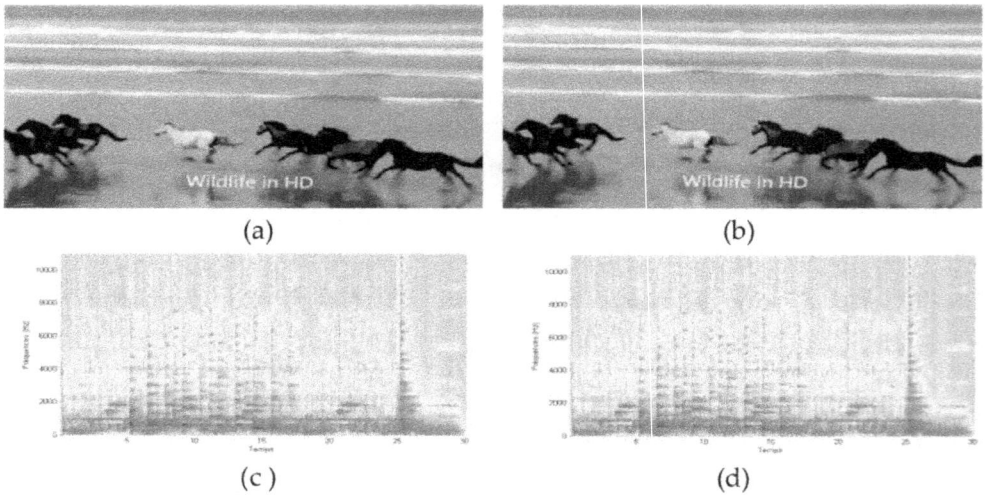

(a)

(b)

(c)

(d)

Figure 10. Video test: "horses.avi"; (a) frame (i) original; (b) frame (i) watermarked; (c) spectrogram of the original audio component; and (d) spectrogram of the watermarked audio component.

3.3. Imperceptibility

Table 2 gives PSNR, UQI, SNR, and ODG values for the imperceptibility tests.

By analyzing and comparing the original image (a) with its watermarked equivalent (b) of the video horses.avi, we notice that they do not present remarkable differences and they are even identical. So the proposed watermarking technique does not affect the quality of images and the inserted brand remains invisible to the human eye. We also note that the spectrogram of figure (c) faithful to that of figure (d). This shows the imperceptible criterion of the technique (**Figure 10**).

From the results in **Table 2**, we note that the PSNR values for video sequences vary between 53.90 and 62.28 dB. These values show that the proposed technique gives very adequate results point of view of imperceptibility of the mark despite the high insertion capacity. These values are highlighted by the values of UQI which vary between 1 and $0.99 \simeq 1$. Similarly for the audio component, we note that the SNR values vary between 62.94 and 68.52 dB, which is very interesting. ODG values further enhance the imperceptible criterion of the technique and they vary between 0 and $- 0.1$. All these values prove the good criterion of imperceptibility guaranteed by the proposed watermarking technique.

3.4. Robustness

To evaluate the robustness, we will apply different types of attacks on the audio and video component of the video: MP3 compression/decompression with the MPEG1 coder "lame.exe" at different compression rates: 128, 96, and 64 kbit/s, the attack by impulsive and Gaussian noise, cropping, frame swapping, frame dropping, frame averaging, and change the coding rate. We will calculate the NC values between the mark before and after the attacks for both components (**Table 3**).

According to the results, we note that the NC values for watermarking system vary between 1 and 0.85 that is very interesting. For values of NC = 1, it means that the mark detected after the attacks is perfectly identical to the initial mark. We also notice that the watermarking system is robust against MPEG1 and MPEG2 compression.

3.5. Comparative analysis

According to the study of the existing, the watermarking techniques for the video watermark only the image component. It is among the contributions of our watermarking system.

In **Table 3**, the notation "−" indicates that data are not available.

Video.avi	128 Kbps	96 Kbps	64 Kbps	MPEG-2	Cropping	Dropping	Swapping	Impulse noise	Gaussian
	NC: audio component			NC: image component					
Windows1	1	1	0.9	0.92	0.97	0.94	0.98	0.93	0.92
WildLife11	−	−	−	0.92	0.91	0.96	0.95	0.85	0.88
Horses	1	0.99	0.95	0.93	0.95	0.90	0.97	0.92	0.91
TV	1	1	0.92	0.85	0.98	0.96	0.96	0.91	0.89
Sample	−	−	−	0.89	0.95	0.90	0.97	0.87	0.9
Foreman	−	−	−	0.9	0.97	0.95	0.97	0.86	0.87

Table 3. NC values.

Techniques	PSNR	MPEG-2	Cropping	Dropping	Swapping	Impulse noise	Gaussian
		NC					
Li and Wang [23]	39.08	0.98	1	—	0.5	—	0.98
Dolley and Manisha [24]	—	0.92	—	0.93	1	0.90	0.41
Supriya and Navin [13]	42.12	—	1	0.98	0.98	0.98	0.98
Shaveta and Daljit [11]	44.88	—	0.91	—	—	0.62	—
Himanshu et al. [25]	—	0.86	0.92	—	0.85	0.69	—
Chitrasen and Tanuja [26]	40.04	—	—	0.59	—	0.50	0.50
Proposed method	60	0.90	0.95	0.93	0.97	0.89	0.89

Table 4. Comparative analysis.

On after PSNR values shown in **Table 4**, we note that the proposed watermarking system guarantees the best criteria of imperceptibility PSNR = 60 dB. In addition, the proposed technique shows good performance against attacks. The NC values vary between 0.89 and 0.97. Comparing the results obtained by the proposed watermarking system with those obtained by Dolley and Manisha in [24], we note that the proposed technique is more robust against the Gaussian attack and for the other attacks, the results are close but from the description of this technique, we found that the detection scheme requires the presence of the original video, while our proposed method requires only the keys which makes the detection faster. In addition, we note that the results obtained by the proposed method are better than those obtained by Chitrasen and Tanuja in [26] which shows the contribution of our watermarking system.

4. Conclusion

In this chapter, we proposed a watermarking system for multimedia documents operating in the frequency domain using MDCT. This watermarking system watermarks both image and audio components, if it exists. For the image component, we injected the message bits into the detected moving object using a motion detection algorithm and in the LSB of the components searched using the Watson model. If the video has an audio component, we have injected the mark in the LSB of the components under the masking curve sought by the psychoacoustic model 2 of the MPEG 1 standard. The imperceptibility of the watermarking system is tested by calculating four measures: PSNR, UQI, ODG, and the SNR. For the image component, we obtained a total PSNR value equal to 60 dB, and an average UQI index equal to $0.99 \cong 1$. For the audio component, we obtained a total SNR value equal to 64.93 dB, and an average ODG value equal to $-0.03 \cong 0$. These values show that the watermarking system ensures a good criterion of imperceptibility. The robustness of the watermarking system is tested by applying several attacks known in the literature as: Gaussian noise, impulse noise, compression MPEG II, MP3 compression,…. The results show the interest of the technique point of view robustness. We obtained NC values between 0.85 and 1.

As a conclusion, we can draw from these obtained results that:

- The frequency domain, in particularly the MDCT, has shown its proof point of view imperceptibility and robustness. There is still a very interesting area.

- The integration of the psychoacoustic model 2 of the MPEG I standard, the use of the Watson model and the motion detection algorithm, the insertion in the LSB, and the Hamming coding improves the performance of the proposed watermarking system.

- We have been able to increase the insertion capacity while maintaining a good criterion of imperceptibility and robustness.

Author details

Maha Bellaaj* and Kaïs Ouni

*Address all correspondence to: maha_bellaaj@yahoo.fr

Research Laboratory Smart Electricity & ICT, SEICT, LR18ES44, National Engineering School of Carthage, ENICarthage, University of Carthage, Tunis, Tunisia

References

[1] Gwenaël D, Jean-Luc D. Problèmatique de la Collusion en Tatouage Vidéo. 2005;**22**(6): 563-574

[2] Hembrooke EF. Identification of sound and like signals. United States Patent: 3,004,104; 1961

[3] Cox I, Miller LM. The first 50 years of electronic watermarking. EURASIP. Journal on Advances in Signal Processing. 2002:126-132. DOI: https://doi.org/10.1155/S1110865702000525

[4] Cléo B. Tatouage informé de signaux audio numériques [thesis]. National School of Telecommunications; 2005

[5] Fadwa D. Tatouage d'images Par Techniques Multidirectionnelles et Multirésolution. [DEA Memory]. National Institute of Applied Sciences of Lyon; 2003

[6] Martin T, Burg J. Digital Representation, Comparison of DCT and DFT. Science of Digital Media; 2007. Supplement to Chapter 4

[7] Marcellin MW, Gormish MJ, Bilgin A, Boliek MP. An overview of JPEG-2000. In: Proceedings of IEEE Data Compression Conference; 2000. pp. 523-541

[8] Sikora T. MPEG digital video coding standards. In: Jurgens R, editor. Digital Consumer Electronics Handbook. New York: McGraw-Hill Book Company; 1997. Chapter 9

[9]   Norme Internationale, ISO/CEI 11172-3. Technologies de l'information codage de l'image animée et du son associé pour les supports de stockage numérique jusqu'à environ 1,5 Mbit/s, partie 3: Audio

[10] Kundur D, Hatzinakos D. Digital watermarking using multiresolution wavelet decomposition. In: Proceedings of IEEE ICASSP '98, Vol. 5. Seattle, WA, USA; 1998. pp. 2969-2972

[11] Shaveta, Daljit K. Scaled wavelet transform video watermarking method using hybrid technique: SWT-SVD-DCT. International Journal of Advanced Technology in Engineering and Science. 2015;**3**(01):78-86. ISSN: 2348-7550

[12] Shital D, Nitin D, Suresh R. Tampering detection and localization in video using fragile watermarking. International Journal of Innovative Research in Computer and Communication Engineering. 2016;**4**(7):13106-13113

[13] Supriya A, Navin S. Digital video watermarking using Dwt and Pca. IOSR Journal of Engineering. 2013;**3**(11):45-49. e-ISSN: 2250-3021, p-ISSN: 2278-8719

[14] Mu-Huo H, Yu-Hsin C. Fast IMDCT and MDCT algorithms—A matrix approach. In: Proceedings of IEEE Transactions on Signal Processing; 2003. pp. 221-229

[15] Delp EJ. Scene Adaptive Video Watermarking. Purdue University School of Electrical and Computer Engineering Purdue Multimedia Testbed. Video and Image Processing Laboratory; 2000

[16] Zlomek M. Video watermarking [thesis]. Charles University in Prague Faculty of Mathematics and Physics; 2007

[17] Peddireddi L. Object Tracking and Velocity Determination Using TMS320C6416T DSK. Klagenfurt: Institute of Networked and Embedded Systems Pervasive Computing; 2008

[18] Weber's Law of Just Noticeable Differences [Internet]. Available from: http://www.usd.edu/psyc301/WebersLaw.htmS [Accessed: August 15, 2016]

[19] Marcellin W, Michael J, Gormish A, Bilgin A, Boliek MP. An overview of JPEG-2000. In: Proceedings of IEEE Data Compression Conference; 2000. pp. 523-541

[20] Hamming RW. Error detecting and error correcting codes. Bell System Technical Journal. 1950;**26**(2):147-160

[21] Union Internationale des Télécommunications (UIT). Recommandation B.S. 1387: Méthode de mesure objective de la qualité du son perçu; 2001

[22] Wang Z, Lu L, Bovik C. Video quality assessment based on structural distortion measurement. Signal Processing: Image Communication. 2004;**19**:121-132

[23] Li X, Wang R. A video watermarking scheme based on 3D-DWT and neural network. In: Proceedings of Ninth IEEE International Symposium on Multimedia; 2007. pp. 110-115

[24] Dolley S, Manisha S. A new approach for scene-based digital video watermarking using discrete wavelet transforms. International Journal of Advanced and Applied Sciences. 2018:148-160

[25] Himanshu A, Rakesh A, Bedi S. Highly robust and imperceptible luminance-based hybrid digital video watermarking scheme for ownership protection. International Journal of Image, Graphics and Signal Processing. 2012;(11):47-52. DOI: 10.5815/ijigsp.2012.11.07

[26] Chitrasen TK. Robust video watermarking using discrete cosine transform and third level discrete wavelet transform. International Journal of Engineering Research and Applications. 2017;7(10.Part-1):87-92. ISSN: 2248-9622

Chapter 3

Color Image Watermarking Based on Radon Transform and Jordan Decomposition

Pranab Kumar Dhar, Rakib Hasan and
Tetsuya Shimamura

Additional information is available at the end of the chapter

http://dx.doi.org/10.5772/intechopen.80407

Abstract

Digital watermarking has been widely used for ownership identification and copyright protection. In this chapter, a color image watermarking method based on Radon transform (RT) and Jordan decomposition (JD) is proposed. Initially, the host color image is converted into L*a*b* color space. Then, the b* channel is selected and it is divided into 16×16 non-overlapping blocks. RT is applied to each of these blocks. JD is applied to the selected RT coefficients of each block represented in $m \times n$ matrix. Watermark data is embedded in the coefficients of the similarity transform matrix obtained from JD using a new quantization equation. Experimental results indicate that the proposed method is highly robust against various attacks such as noise addition, cropping, filtering, blurring, rotation, JPEG compression etc. In addition, it provides high quality watermarked images. Moreover, it shows superior performance than the state-of-the-art methods reported recently in terms of imperceptibility and robustness.

Keywords: imperceptibility, quantization, Jordan decomposition, radon transform, robustness

1. Introduction

Internet is the fastest growing medium of transferring data to any place in the world. The creation and distribution of digital media content is increasing day by day. With the recent proliferation of the internet, the threat of privacy and copyright of digital content has become an important issue. Digital watermarking is the most secured way to protect copyright protection and authentication.

Various types of image watermarking methods have been proposed in past decades. Two types of watermarking techniques are used according to domain [1]. In the spatial domain techniques, the watermark is embedded in the pixel values of an image. Least significant bit (LSB) watermarking is the most common spatial domain embedding technique. It is not an effective way to embed watermark because the watermark can be easily removed or modified. In transform domain techniques, the watermark is embedded into the coefficients of the transformed domain. Discrete wavelet transform (DWT), discrete cosine transform (DCT) and discrete Fourier transform (DFT) are the most common transformations that are utilized in transform domain techniques. A novel blind watermarking algorithm in DCT domain using the correlation between two DCT coefficients of adjacent blocks in the same position is proposed by Das et al. [2]. Sadreazami et al. [3] used a blind watermarking scheme in the wavelet-based contourlet domain. For embedding, they used an even-odd quantization technique. A multipurpose image watermarking scheme is proposed by Ansari and Pant [4] in order to provide tamper localization, self-recovery and ownership verification of the host image. Choudhary and Parmar [5] introduced a robust image watermarking technique using two-level DWT. However, the peak signal-to-noise-ratio (PSNR) is quite low and they did not assess the robustness against malicious attack. Recently, singular value decomposition (SVD) has been widely used in image watermarking. Siddiqui and Kaur [6] proposed a hybrid method based on DWT and SVD. The robustness of this method is good but the PSNR of the watermarked image is little low. Another DWT and SVD-based image watermarking method is presented by Srilakshmi and Himabindu [7]. The PSNR of this method is good but the robustness against attacks is low. Savakar and Ghuli [8] proposed multiple methods such as single level DWT, DFT, SVD to embed watermark. The PSNR of this method is quite low.

Very few papers utilized Radon transform (RT) in watermarking. Siddik and Elbasi [9] introduced a watermarking technique using RT. Rastegar et al. [10] proposed a hybrid watermarking algorithm based on RT and SVD. They also used 2D-DWT in the RT domain. The PSNR of this method is good but robustness of this method against malicious attacks is low. To overcome the limitations, in this chapter, we propose an image watermarking method based on RT and Jordan decomposition (JD). To the best of our knowledge, this is the first image watermarking method based RT and JD. The main features of the proposed method include (i) it utilizes the RT, JD and quantization jointly, (ii) the watermark bits are embedded into the similarity transform matrix of the RT coefficients obtained from b channel of the original host image using a new quantization equation, (iii) it provides high robustness against various attacks as well as good quality watermarked images, and (iv) it achieves a good trade-off between imperceptibility and robustness (v) it shows superior performance than the state-of-the-art methods in terms of imperceptibility and robustness. The peak signal-to-noise ratio (PSNR) and structural similarity (SSIM) of the proposed method range from 47.4997 to 51.8848 and 0.9989 to 0.9998, respectively. On the other hand, PSNR and SSIM of the recent methods [4, 11] range from 29.5667 to 34.4495 and 0.9507 to 0.9907, respectively. The normalized correlation (NC) of the proposed method for various attacks ranges from 0.9939 to 1, in contrast to the recent methods whose NC range from 0.0020 to 0.9996.

The rest of the chapter is organized as follows. Section 2 provides a background information including RT and JD. The proposed watermarking method is introduced in Section 3. Section 4 compares the performance of the proposed method with some recent methods in terms of imperceptibility and robustness. Finally, Section 5 concludes this chapter.

2. Background information

2.1. Radon transform (RT)

Johann Radon invented RT in 1917 also provided the formula for the inverse transform (**Figure 1**). The Radon transform is an integral transform that takes a function f defined on the plane to a function R_f defined on the (two-dimensional) space of lines in the plane. Its value at a particular line is equal to the line integral of the function over that line [12].

The Radon transform can be expressed as follows:

$$Rf(\alpha, s) = \int_{-\infty}^{\infty} f(x(z), y(z))dz$$
$$= \int_{-\infty}^{\infty} f((z \sin \alpha + s \cos \alpha), (-z \cos \alpha + s \sin \alpha))dz$$

(1)

After applying inverse radon transform, we can reconstruct the original image quite well. RT has been widely used in various applications of image processing. RT has excellent feature to

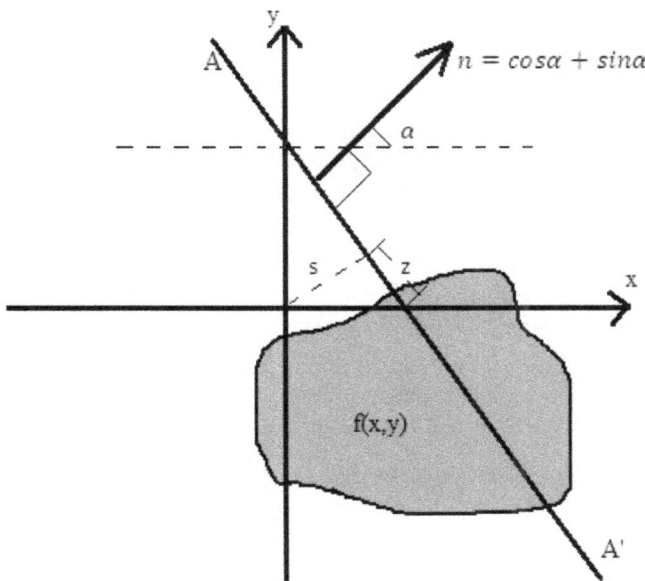

Figure 1. Radon transform that maps f on the (x,y) domain to the (α, s) domain.

transform the information from two-dimensional image into a string of one-dimensional projections which is computationally faster. It has the following advantages:

i.   It has the ability to detect line width and has good robustness for noisy images.

ii.   If the image scaled as angle θ, RT is also changed according to same size

$$I(x \cos \phi - y \sin \phi + y \cos \phi) \leftrightarrow R(x, \theta + \phi).$$

iii. If image resized as p, RT is also change with same size

$$I(px, py) \leftrightarrow \frac{1}{p} R(pX, \theta)$$

RT produces a big matrix by computing projections of an image along specified direction. For this reason, there is very little effect of embedding watermark in RT domain, which provides high quality watermarked images as well as good robustness against various attacks.

2.2. Jordan decomposition

Jordan decomposition (also known as Jordan normal form or Jordan canonical form) results from the conversion of a matrix into its diagonal form by a similarity transformation [13]. The Jordan matrix decomposition of a square matrix A can be represented by:

$$A = VJV^{-1} \tag{2}$$

Here, the Jordan normal form J is the diagonal matrix of eigenvalues and the similarity transform matrix V contains the generalized eigenvectors as columns. The use of similarity transform aims at reducing the complexity of the problem of evaluating the eigenvalues of a matrix. Indeed, if a given matrix could be transformed into a similar matrix in diagonal form, the computation of the eigenvalues would be easy. Moreover, the slight variations of eigenvalues in embedding watermark have little effect on the quality of the watermarked image. For this reason, it provides high quality watermarked images as well as good robustness against various attacks.

3. Proposed watermarking method

Let $I = \{i(u, v), 1 \le u \le M, 1 \le v \le M\}$ be the host image and $W = \{w(k, l), 1 \le k \le N, 1 \le j \le N\}$ be a binary watermark image to be embedded into the host image.

The proposed watermarking method is described in this section which can be divided into two parts (i) watermark embedding process and (ii) watermark extraction process.

3.1. Watermark embedding process

The watermark embedding process is shown in **Figure 2** and it can be stated as follows:

1. The original host image I is converted into L*a*b* color space denoted by I_L, I_a, and I_b.

2. The I_b channel is selected and this channel is divided into $n \times n$ non-overlapping blocks denoted by B_a with a border size of 1×1.

3. RT is applied on each block B_a of the color space I_b. After applying RT, transformed matrix R_b is obtained.

4. JD is applied to a part of the matrix R_b of size $p \times p$ denoted by R_{bs}. This is because computational cost of JD is quite high and it takes long time to perform on a big matrix. The JD can be represented as follows:

$$R_{bs} = V_C J_C V_C^{-1} \tag{3}$$

Here, Jc is the Jordan normal form and Vc is the similarity transform matrix.

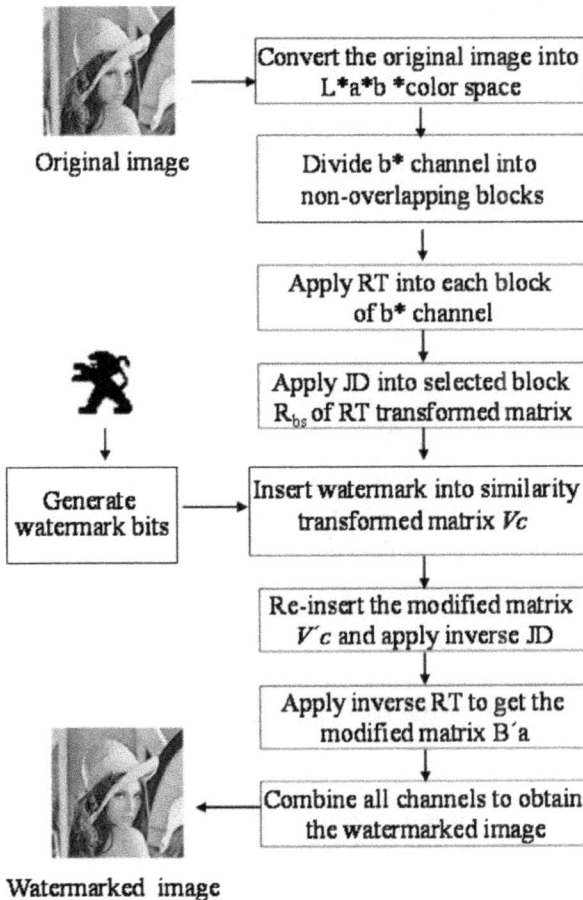

Figure 2. Watermark embedding process.

5. In order to guarantee the robustness and imperceptibility, the proposed algorithm embeds watermark bit into all coefficients of similarity transform matrix V_C using a new quantization function. This ensures that the watermark is located at the most significant perceptual components of the image. Watermark data is embedded by using the following equation:

$$V_C'(i,j) = \begin{cases} V_C(i,j) + \dfrac{\text{Bmod}(q)}{V_{\max} \times \Delta} + (V_{\max} \times \Delta) \, if \, W(k,l) = 1 \\ V_C(i,j) - \Delta \, if \, W(k,l) = 0 \end{cases} \tag{4}$$

where, B is the current block number, q is an integer, Δ is an integer, V_{max} is the maximum value of matrix V_C.

6. Reinsert each modified coefficient $V_c'(i, j)$ into matrix V_c' and inverse JD is applied to obtain the modified matrix R'_{bs}.

7. Reinsert each modified matrix R'_{bs} into R_b to obtain modified matrix R'_b.

8. Inverse RT is applied to each modified matrix R'_b to get the modified block B'_a.

9. All modified blocks are combined to obtain the modified color space $I_{b'}$.

10. Finally, all the channels I_{L*}, I_{a*}, and I'_{b*} are combined to get the watermarked image I'.

3.2. Watermark extraction process

In watermark extraction process, both the original host image I and attacked watermarked image I^* are used, which is shown in **Figure 3** and can be described as follows:

1. The original host image I and attacked watermarked image I^* are converted into L*a*b* color space denoted by I_L, I_a, I_b and I^*_L, I^*_a, I^*_b, respectively.

2. The I_b and I^*_b channel of I and I^* are selected and divided into $n \times n$ non-overlapping blocks denoted by B_a and B^*_a, respectively with a border size of 1×1.

3. RT is applied on each block B_a and B^*_a of the color space I_b and I'_b, respectively. After applying RT, transformed matrix R_b and R^*_b are obtained.

4. JD is applied to a part of the matrix R_b and R^*_b of size $p \times p$ denoted by R_{bs} and R^*_{bs} to obtain the two Jordan matrices J_C, J_C^* and two similarity transform matrices V_C, V_C^*, respectively.

5. To extract the watermark bits, the transform matrices V_C and V_C^* are compared. If the selected coefficients extracted from V_C^* is less than or equal to that of V_C, then the extracted watermark bit will be '0'. Otherwise, the extracted watermark bit will be '1'. This can be expressed as follows:

$$W^*(k,l) = \begin{cases} 0 \, if \, V_C^*(k,l) \leq V_C(k,l) \\ 1 \, otherwise \end{cases} \tag{5}$$

where $V_C(k,l)$ and $V_C^*(k,l)$ are the extracted value from the original and attacked watermarked image and $W^*(k,l)$ is the extracted watermark bit.

6. After extracting all the watermark bits, the binary watermark image W^* is obtained.

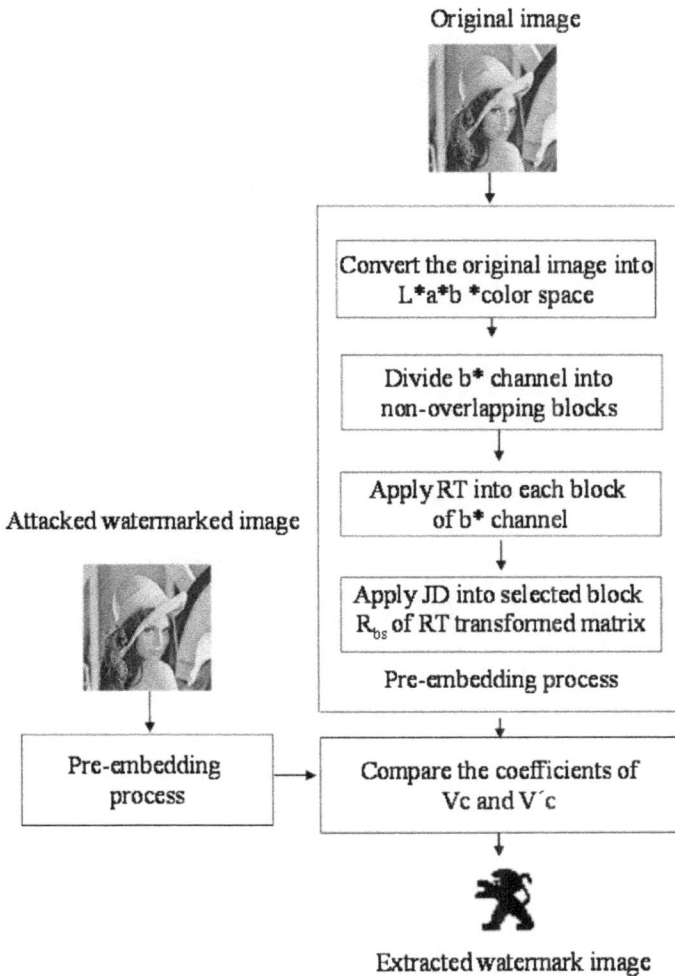

Figure 3. Watermark extraction process.

4. Experimental results

In this section, we have evaluated the performance of our proposed method in terms of imperceptibility and robustness. We carried out several experiments and also compared with some recent methods. In this study, we used four color JPEG images of size 256×256 from the USC-SIPI image database [14] shown in **Figure 4**. The binary watermark image of size 32×32 is used in our experiment taken from the Free Stencil Gallery [15] shown in **Figure 5**. In this study, for simplicity the selected value for n and p are 16 and 2, respectively. Computational cost of JD is quite high and it takes long time to perform JD on a big matrix. For this reason, we have selected a small value for p.

(a)   (b)

(c)   (d)

Figure 4. Host images used in our experiment (a) airplane, (b) Lena, (c) house, and (d) baboon.

Figure 5. Watermark image use in our experiment.

4.1. Imperceptibility

To test the imperceptibility of the proposed method, we have calculated peak signal-to-noise ratio (PSNR) and structural similarity index measurement (SSIM) watermarked images.

PSNR is calculated using the following equation:

$$PSNR = 10 \log_{10} \left(\frac{255^2}{\frac{1}{MM} \sum_{k=1}^{M} \sum_{l=1}^{M} \left(A - A' \right)^2} \right) \tag{6}$$

The watermarked images are shown in **Figure 6**.

(a) (b)

(c) (d)

Figure 6. Watermarked images obtained in this experiment (a) airplane, (b) Lena, (c) house, and (d) baboon.

SSIM is an efficient method for measuring the similarity between two images and it can be expressed as:

$$SSIM(A, A') = \frac{(2\mu_I\mu_{I'} + c_1)(2\sigma_{II'} + c_2)}{(\mu_I^2 + \mu_{I'}^2 + c_1)(\sigma_I^2 + \sigma_{I'}^2 + c_2)} \tag{7}$$

Here, μ_I, σ_I, $\mu_{I'}$, $\sigma_{I'}$, and $\sigma_{II'}$ indicate the mean of I, variance of I, mean of I', variance of I', covariance of I and I', respectively. c_1, and c_2 are the two variables used in Eq. (7).

Table 1 shows the PSNR comparison between the proposed scheme and two recent methods. Ansari and Pant [4] used DWT-SVD domain to embed watermark. This method has an average PSNR value of 34.4356. Al-Afandy et al. [11] used discrete stationary wavelet transform (DSWT) in the DCT domain to embed watermark. This method has an average PSNR value of 33.1474 and ranges from 29 to 36. This is in contrast to the proposed method whose PSNR values ranges from 47.4997 to 51.8848 and the average value is 49.0387.

Table 1 also shows the SSIM comparison between the proposed scheme and two recent methods. The more the SSIM value approaches to 1, the better the image quality is. Our proposed method provides SSIM values close to 1 which is excellent for a watermarked image. Also, the proposed method shows higher SSIM values compared to the recent methods.

Radon transform generates a large matrix from the given image matrix which is convenient for embedding watermark. For this reason, we have used a small portion of transformed matrix for watermark insertion. Hence, there is very little effect on embedding watermark into the host image and we obtained higher PSNR, SSIM values compared to the conventional methods.

Image	Measurement	Ansari and Pant [4]	Al-Afandy et al. [11]	Proposed
Airplane	PSNR	34.4495	33.6072	49.2705
	SSIM	0.9672	0.9507	0.9989
Lena	PSNR	34.4339	34.2382	51.8848
	SSIM	0.9701	0.9907	0.9998
House	PSNR	34.4196	35.1776	47.4997
	SSIM	0.9694	0.9833	0.9995
Baboon	PSNR	34.4393	29.5667	47.4997
	SSIM	0.9889	0.9529	0.9993
Ave range	PSNR	49.0387	33.1474	49.0387
	SSIM	0.9889	0.9529	0.9993

Table 1. Comparison between the proposed scheme and several recent methods in terms of PSNR and SSIM.

4.2. Robustness

To assess the robustness, we have calculated normalized correlation (NC) which computes the difference between original watermark and the extracted watermark. The equation of NC is given below:

$$NC(W, W^*) = \frac{\sum_{k=1}^{N} \sum_{l=1}^{N} w(k, l) \cdot w^*(k, l)}{\sqrt{\sum_{k=1}^{N} \sum_{l=1}^{N} w(k, l) \cdot w(k, l)} \sqrt{\sum_{k=1}^{N} \sum_{l=1}^{N} w^*(k, l) \cdot w^*(k, l)}} \tag{8}$$

where k and l are the indices of the binary watermark image. The correlation between W and W^* is very high when NC (W, W^*) is close to 1. On the other hand, the correlation between W and W^* is very low when NC (W, W^*) is close to zero.

From **Figure 7**, we observed that NC varies when quantization step size Δ is below 6. NC remains constant at 1 when $\Delta \geq 6$. In this study, the selected value for Δ is 15.

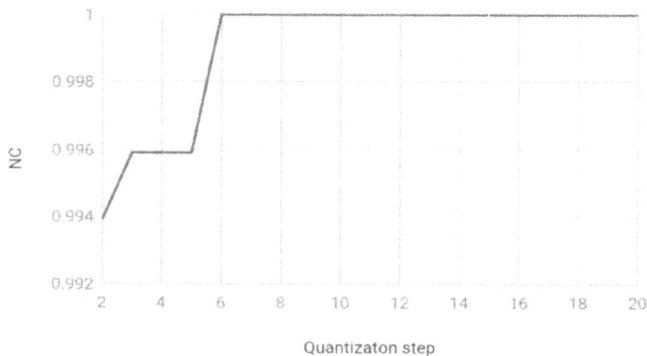

Figure 7. NC vs. quantization step size.

Figure 8. Different types of attacks applied to watermarked image 'Lena' (a) JPEG(30), (b) JPEG(90), (c) JPEG 2000, (d) salt & pepper noise, (e) Gaussian white noise, (f) speckle noise, (g) median filter, (h) wiener filter, (i) crop (25%) (j) rotation 25°, (j) sharpened, and (k) blurred.

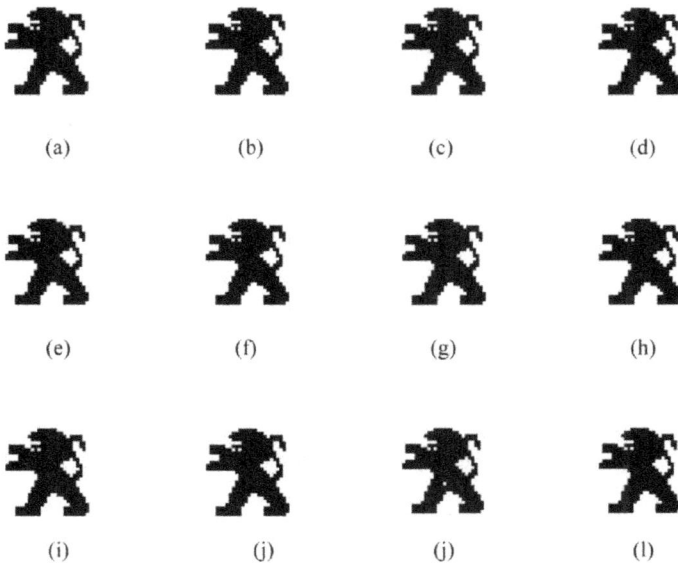

Figure 9. Extracted watermark image after applying various attacks on 'Lena' image (a) JPEG(30), (b) JPEG(90), (c) JPEG 2000, (d) salt & pepper noise, (e) Gaussian white noise, (f) speckle noise, (g) median filter, (h) wiener filter, (i) crop (25%), (j) rotation 25°, (j) sharpened, and (k) blurred.

To verify the robustness of our proposed method, we applied different malicious attacks such as noise addition, cropping, rotation, filtering, blurring, sharpening, JPEG compression etc. on the watermarked image. **Figure 8** shows the effects of attacks on the watermarked image 'Lena'. We can also observe the watermark image extracted from the attacked watermarked image in **Figure 9**. From this figures, we observed that our proposed method shows high robustness against various attacks. **Tables 2** and **3** show the NC comparison between the proposed scheme and several recent methods against various attacks. The method proposed by Ansari and Pant [4] show good robustness where NC values range from 0.0020 to 0.9961. But, this method cannot resist against cropping and rotation attack. The method proposed by Al-Afandy et al. [11] proposed method shows good robustness and the NC values of this range

Attack	Images	Proposed	Ansari and Pant [4]	Al-Afandy et al. [11]
JPEG(30)	Airplane	1	0.9689	0.9997
	Lena	1	0.9702	0.9997
	House	0.9980	0.9685	0.9995
	Baboon	1	0.9961	0.9998
JPEG(90)	Airplane	1	0.9956	0.9998
	Lena	1	0.9956	0.9997
	House	0.9980	0.9957	0.9995
	Baboon	1	0.9953	0.9997
JPEG 2000	Airplane	1	0.9955	0.9998
	Lena	1	0.9955	0.9997
	House	0.9980	0.9957	0.9995
	Baboon	1	0.9951	0.9998
Salt and pepper noise	Airplane	0.9980	0.6008	0.9991
	Lena	1	0.5895	0.9973
	House	0.9959	0.6373	0.9992
	Baboon	1	0.6236	0.9984
Gaussian white noise	Airplane	0.9980	0.7293	0.9992
	Lena	1	0.7453	0.9963
	House	0.9959	0.7158	0.9992
	Baboon	1	0.7284	0.9989
Speckle noise	Airplane	1	0.4654	0.9994
	Lena	1	0.6181	0.9991
	House	0.9939	0.5542	0.9996
	Baboon	1	0.6099	0.9993
Median filter	Airplane	1	0.9961	0.9996

Table 2. NC comparison between the proposed scheme and several methods against various noise and JPEG compression attacks.

Attack	Images	Proposed	Ansari and Pant [4]	Al-Afandy et al. [11]
Median filtering	Airplane	1	0.9961	0.9996
	Lena	1	0.9960	0.9996
	House	0.9980	0.9961	0.9994
	Baboon	1	0.9956	0.9993
Wiener filtering	Airplane	0.9980	0.9961	0.9996
	Lena	1	0.9960	0.9996
	House	1	0.9961	0.9994
	Baboon	1	0.9956	0.9995
Cropping 25%	Airplane	1	0.0707	0.9997
	Lena	1	0.0551	0.9996
	House	0.9980	0.0588	0.9994
	Baboon	1	0.0020	0.9996
Rotation 25°	Airplane	1	0.0216	0.9974
	Lena	1	0.0738	0.9981
	House	0.9980	0.0155	0.9983
	Baboon	1	0.0715	0.9990
Sharpening	Airplane	1	0.9748	0.9996
	Lena	0.9980	0.9762	0.9983
	House	0.9959	0.9802	0.9996
	Baboon	1	0.9755	0.9977
Blurring	Airplane	1	0.5738	0.9994
	Lena	1	0.6673	0.9993
	House	0.9980	0.6496	0.9992
	Baboon	1	0.7478	0.9990

Table 3. NC comparison between the proposed scheme and several methods against filtering, cropping, rotation. sharpening, and blurring attacks.

from 0.9977 to 0.9997. Our proposed method shows higher NC values than these method against various attacks. This is because watermark is embedded into the similarity transform matrix of the RT coefficients obtained from b channel of the original host image using a new quantization equation.

5. Conclusions

In this chapter, we have introduced a color image watermarking method based on RT and JD. Simulation results demonstrate that the proposed method is highly robust against different attacks such as noise addition, cropping, filtering, rotation, blurring, sharpening, and JPEG compression. In addition, it provides high quality watermarked images. Moreover, it outperforms state-of-the-art image watermarking methods in terms of imperceptibility and robustness. These results indicate that the proposed watermarking method can be used for image copyright protection.

Author details

Pranab Kumar Dhar[1]*, Rakib Hasan[1] and Tetsuya Shimamura[2]

*Address all correspondence to: pranabdhar81@gmail.com

1 Department of Computer Science and Engineering, Chittagong University of Engineering and Technology (CUET), Chittagong, Bangladesh

2 Graduate School of Science and Engineering, Saitama University, Saitama, Japan

References

[1] Tyagi S, Singh HV, Agarwal R, Gangwar SK. Digital watermarking techniques for security applications. In: 2016 International Conference on Emerging Trends in Electrical Electronics & Sustainable Energy Systems (ICETEESES); 2016

[2] Das C, Panigrahi S, Sharma VK, Mahapatra K. A novel blind robust image watermarking in DCT domain using inter-block coefficient correlation. AEU - International Journal of Electronics and Communications. 2014;**68**(3):244-253

[3] Sadreazami H, Ahmad MO, Swamy MNS. A robust quantization-based image watermarking scheme in the wavelet-based contourlet domain. In: 2016 IEEE Canadian Conference on Electrical and Computer Engineering (CCECE); 2016

[4] Ansari A, Pant M. Multipurpose image watermarking in the domain of DWT based on SVD and ABC. Pattern Recognition Letters. 2017;**94**:228-236

[5] Choudhary R, Parmar G. A robust image watermarking technique using 2-level discrete wavelet transform (DWT). In: 2016 2nd International Conference on Communication Control and Intelligent Systems (CCIS); 2016

[6] Siddiqui A, Kaur A. A secure and robust image watermarking system using wavelet domain. In: 2017 7th International Conference on Cloud Computing, Data Science & Engineering - Confluence; 2017

[7] Srilakshmi P, Himabindu C. Image watermarking with path based selection using DWT & SVD. In: 2016 IEEE International Conference on Computational Intelligence and Computing Research (ICCIC); 2016

[8] Savakar DG, Ghuli A. Non-blind digital watermarking with enhanced image embedding capacity using DMeyer wavelet decomposition, SVD, and DFT. Pattern Recognition and Image Analysis. 2017;**27**(3):511-517

[9] Siddik O, Elbasi E. Information hiding: A new multi watermark algorithm using radon transformation. International Journal of Information and Electronics Engineering. 2015; **5**(6):460-463

[10] Rastegar S, Namazi F, Yaghmaie K, Aliabadian A. Hybrid watermarking algorithm based on singular value decomposition and radon transform. AEU - International Journal of Electronics and Communications. 2011;**65**(7):658-663

[11] Al-Afandy KA, Faragallah OS, El-Rabaie E-S M, El-Samie FEA, Elmhalawy A. A hybrid scheme for robust color image watermarking using DSWT in DCT domain. In: 2016 4th IEEE International Colloquium on Information Science and Technology (CiSt); 2016

[12] Radon Transform. Wikipedia [Online]. Available from: https://en.wikipedia.org/wiki/Radon_transform

[13] Documentation. Jordan Canonical Form - MATLAB & Simulink [Online]. Available from: https://www.mathworks.com/help/symbolic/jordan-canonical-form.html

[14] The USC-SIPI Image Database [Online]. Available from: http://sipi.usc.edu/database/

[15] Peugeot Logo Stencil. Free Stencil Gallery [Online]. Available from: http://www.freestencilgallery.com/peugeot-logo-stencil

Steganography

Detection of Motion Vector-Based Video Steganography by Adding or Subtracting One Motion Vector Value

Srinivas Bachu and Aravind Kumar Madam

Additional information is available at the end of the chapter

http://dx.doi.org/10.5772/intechopen.78230

Abstract

In last decades the Steganography is an tremendous progress, at the same time there exist issues to detect the steganalysis in motion based video where the substance is reliably in motion conduct that makes that to detect it. Analyzing the difference between the rated motion value plays a crucial role that enables us to focus on difference between the locally optimal SAD and actual SAD after adding-or-subtracting-one operation on the motion value. Based on the motion vectors to play out the classification and extraction process at last, two features sets are been used based on the fact that most motion vectors are locally optimal for most video codec's to complete this process. The conventional approaches announced the technique for proposed prevails to meet the requirement applications and detecting the steganalysis in videos compare in the literature.

Keywords: adaptive filters, SNR, MSE, LMS, NLMS

1. Introduction

To detect the presence of secretly hidden data in an object is the main objective of steganalysis. Video, audio and images are digital media file that are ideal cover object for steganography to install a secret message. By using measurable descriptor, some empirical spreads are somewhat difficult to show precisely besides which considerably confuses recognition of embedding changes. From cover and stego objects the location can't be founded on assessments of the basic probability distributions of statistics removed except for a couple of pathological cases. Rather, detection is normally given a role as a classification administered issue executed by utilizing machine learning [1].

Although there exists an extensive variety of different machine learning tools, support vector machines (SVMs) appear to be by a wide margin the most popular choice. This is because of the way that SVMs are upheld by a strong mathematical cost inside the statistical learning hypothesis and based on the fact that they are impervious to overtraining and per-outlines rather well despite when the element dimensionality is identical or greater than the traverse of the training set. Moreover, executions of productive open source are available for download and utilize easy.

The SVM training complexity, however, development cycle slows down even for the issue of moderate size, as the complexity of calculating the Gram Matrix representing the kernel is proportional to the square of the product of feature dimensionality and the size of training set. Moreover, in the number of samples training at least quadratics is itself in training. To the analysis the ensemble classifier give more freedom, without constrain on feature dimensionality who can now design the feature virtually and the size of training set through a much faster development cycle to build detectors.

Based on the steganalysis algorithm early features used just a few dozen features, e.g., discrete cosine transform (DCT) features, changing an image utilizing higher request snapshots of wavelet coefficient, quadratic mirror filter and binary similarity metric of 72 higher request snapshots of coefficients got. With the desire the increased sophistication of steganography algorithm, to use the feature vector of increasingly higher vector dimensionality to detect steganography more accurately prompted steganalyst. The set of feature designed for the images JPEG portrayed in utilized features and twice its size by Cartesian calibration was later stretched out, while feature vector dimensionality of 324-and 486 were proposed in and individually. The pixel difference in the second-order Markov model spam set has a dimensionality of 686. Additionally, it builds beneficial computed from different domain to merge features to increase further diversity. In a key dependent domain the dimensionality of 1234 cross-domain features (CDF) set demonstrated particularly successful against YA that make embedding changes.

Various number of Eigen vectors are selected by utilizing different systems. The Eigen vectors are supplanted to enhance the accuracy and also the data compression is done based on the largest K Eigen value. The FERET (Facial Recognition Technology) database was created by Moon and Phillips (1998) to estimate and compare the single step of the face recognition approach. The experimental results of present work presenting the comparisons distance measure over the real time results of the trained set of images, videos [2].

1.1. Cryptography

The process of the methods such cryptography and the steganography both are almost same. In existing, those methods have the wider area but now, the recently developed method is the sub domain of the existing one. Here, the original sensitive information's are encrypted by utilizing the cryptography method. This encrypted information's are hard to recognize by others. These methods are also known as the interrelated process, here, initially, the sensitive information's are encrypted then the stego-tool is utilized to hide the encrypted data. Compared with other methods, the stego-tool is worked efficiently to hide the sensitive data [2, 3]. In the cryptography process, the information's are shared in a secret manner or chippers between the users. **Figure 1** shows the process of the cryptography method.

Plain text is the data or original message as input that is fed into the algorithm. By using any cryptographic algorithm the process of Encryption that modifies the plain text as cipher text. The encrypted message of the cipher text is the mix of the secret key and the original message. Using a secret key to get the original plain text decryption is the reverse process of encryption is used. Without using key for gathering original information of the cipher text cryptanalysis is the way to study the methods. To produce original plaintext the algorithm of decryption takes the secret key and cipher text.

From unauthorized persons to conceal the information the first raw message, alluded to as plaintext, is changed over into a random cipher text. To be changed the original message is said as text plain, from the change the message coming about is the text cipher. A plain content into a cipher text the procedure of is called encryption. The Decryption is the reverse process. The process of encryption contains a key and algorithm. The algorithm is controlled by key.

To design an encryption technique is the objective that would be impossible or very difficult for an unauthorized party. By using the secret key, a user can recover the original message only by decrypting the cipher text. The algorithm will create different output depending upon the secret key. The output of the algorithm changes if the secret key changes.

The conventional encryption security depends on several factors. The algorithm of encryption must be intense. The message of the decryption ought to be troublesome. The algorithm is dependent on the secrecy of the key. To keep it secret in this way, it is mandatory.

The message is denoted as A and the k is denoted as encryption key, the process of encryption will be write as,

$$B = En\,(K, A). \tag{1}$$

$$A = De\,(K, B). \tag{2}$$

Here the cipher text is meant as B. With key K to encrypt the message An En is a capacity. The opposite procedure of description DE is the En encryption.

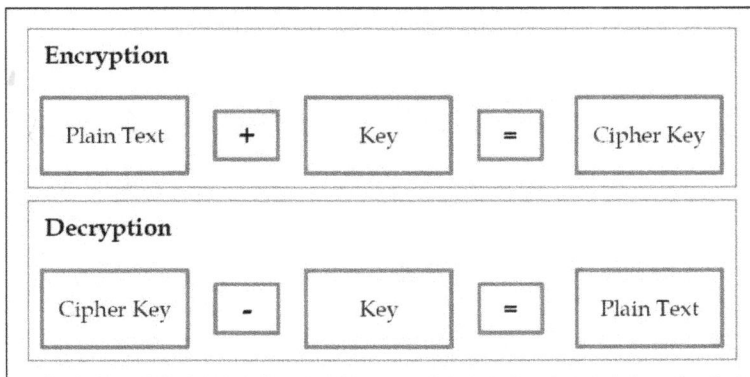

Figure 1. Process of cryptography.

$$\text{Example :}\quad \text{Plain text } (X) = \text{This is a sample text, } K = \text{strrev}(X)$$
$$\text{Cipher text } (Y) = \text{txet elpmas a si siht.}\tag{3}$$

To K or X watching, Y yet not approaching an opponent, will attempt to recuperate K and X. It is accepted that the Opponent has learning of the decryption (De) and encryption (En) algorithms.

1.2. Steganography

The process of the Steganography is, the sensitive information about the audio of the video file is hiding and the hided information is not hacked and seen by other unknown persons. If the unknown persons try to hack the crypted data, they are confused, because both the cryptography and the steganography methods have the same process to hide the sensitive information. Nevertheless, the steganography is efficient method because the data are encrypted without knowing others.

The term Steganography is taken from Greek word. The words Steganos and graptos are combined to form the term Steganography. The meaning of 'Steganos' is the covered and the meaning of 'graptos' is the writing. By using this method, the digital information is converted into audio or video files. The inverse process of the Steganography is known as the Steganalysis. The concealed data are detected by using this Steganalysis (**Figure 2**).

1.3. Video steganography

Among the different kinds of steganography the video steganography is one of the variants of steganography. The info media is a video document in video steganography. The video steganography forms are appeared in **Figure 3**.

Signature is the message original that is fed into the cover media. As the cover media the video frames are taken. Key is the method for organizing divided computerized signature into the cover media. Utilizing any cryptographic algorithm the procedure of encryption is arranging

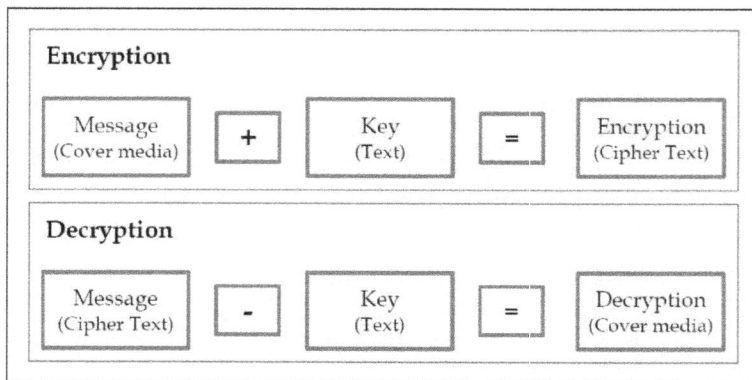

Figure 2. Process of steganography.

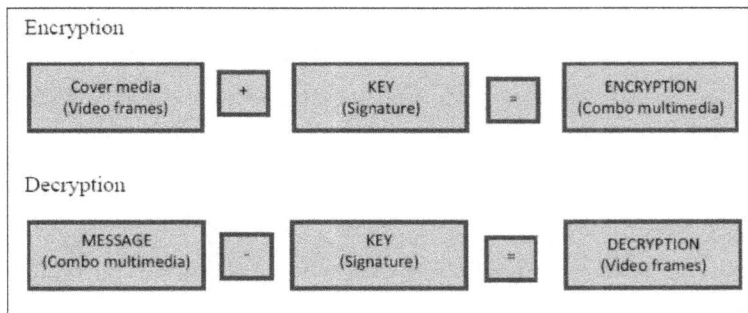

Figure 3. Process of video steganography.

partitioned digital signature into the cover media. The secret key and the first message are the mix of cipher data. Utilizing secret key to get original information the decryption is the inverse process of encryption, which is used.

2. Literature survey

In 2004 for binary images a basic data hiding technique was proposed by Liu and Chang [4]. At the edge part of host binary image the proposed strategy installs secure data. To discover the edge pixels of host binary image the distance matrix mechanism is utilized. For picking the most appropriate one to consider the network of the neighborhood around alterable pixels then the weight mechanism is utilized. To appropriate the embedding data into the general image an irregular number generator is utilized for the security and quality thought. These technique not just implants a lot of data into host binary image yet additionally can keep up quality of image.

In 2005 in view of pixel value differencing (PVD) and least significant bit (LSB) Replacement strategies a novel stenographic strategy was proposed by Wu et al. [5] so as to give am imperceptible stego quality of image and to enhance the capacity of the shrouded secret data. To segregate between smooth areas and edge areas of cover image the pixel value differencing (PVD) strategy is utilized. By LSB technique the secret data is covered up into the smooth areas of cover image in the edge areas while utilizing the PVD strategy. In the edge areas the proposed techniques store data as well as in smooth areas in this manner it can conceal considerably bigger data and keeps up a decent visual nature of stego picture.

A no-reference video quality metric that aimlessly assesses the quality of a video was proposed by Carli et al. [6] in 2005. To embed a fragile check into perceptually critical zones of the video frames they had utilized block based spread spectrum embedding strategy. To describe the perceptual significance of a region they utilized an arrangement of perceptual features that are color, contrast and motion. On receiver side from the perceptually essential territories of the decoded video the check is extricated. By figuring the degradation of the extracted check ther.

a quality measure of the video is acquired. On perceptually critical areas of the video frame by utilizing basic embedding system along these lines quality of a compressed video is assessed.

In binary image a novel strategy for hidden data was proposed by Tseng et al. [7] in 2007. For turning to choose the most appropriate pixel a weight mechanism is utilized. To counteract boundary distortion and to enhance the visual quality of stego image, the boundary check is performed. For watermarked image this strategy accomplished a decent visual quality and has embedding high capacity.

Utilizing minimum significant piece to hide data in a colorful image a novel technique was proposed and all in all the art and science of steganography was talked about by Mehboob and Faruqui [8] in 2008. After the header this technique cleaves the data in 8 bits and to hide data utilized LSB. For hiding data so they demonstrated LSB strategy is the most suggested than alternate techniques that require filtering and masking.

In 2010, LSB substitution and on four pixel differencing for gray level images a novel steno-graphic strategy was proposed by Ould Medeniand and El Mamoun Souidi [9]. In the most piece of the pixel where K is chosen by the quantity of one for hiding the secrete data into the every pixel they utilized K-bit LSB substitution technique. For the PSNR measure this strategy gave best values, which imply that there were no enormous distinction between the stegno and original image.

To execute a strong dynamic technique for data hiding to make stegnalysis a convoluted undertaking and additionally to enhance the capacity of the secret data assignment they tried in view of PVD and LSB substitution a data hiding strategy was proposed by Mahjabin et al. [10] in 2012. dynamic embedding and efficient algorithm was proposed with an imperceptible visual quality here that not just shrouds secret data and capacity expanded for the attackers yet in addition make mystery code breaking a decent irritation. Lower image degradation and an increased embedding capacity accomplished this strategy with enhanced security when contrasted with the substitution technique LSB and a few data hiding existing strategy.

In 2012 in RGB lossless images for hiding text messages an enhanced stenography approach was proposed by Ankit Chaudhary and JaJdeep Vasavada [11]. Inside specific image portions by randomly appropriating the instant message over the entire image as opposed to clustering the security level is expanded. For storing data by using all the color channels they expanded storage capacity and giving the compression of source text message. For hiding the message by changing just a single rent critical piece per color channel the degradation of the images can be limited, in the original image causing a next to no change. In this way, while acquiring minimal quality degradation this strategy enhanced the capacity and expanded the security level.

In 2012 for video stenography a secured has based LSB technique was proposed by Dasgupta and Mandaland Paramartha Dutta [12]. To disguise the nearness of sensitive data paying little heed to its arrangement in spatial domain this system uses cover video files. With LSB tech-nique in the wake of looking at the proposed technique it is discovered that the execution examination of proposed technique is quite reassuring. In multiple frames as the message can be embedded in video stenography the upside of this technique is that the span of the message does not make a difference.

To recover the hidden information and in computer video file to hide data containing content a strategy was proposed by Bodhak and Gunjal [13] in 2012. Utilizing DCT and LSB Modification strategy in a video file such that the video does not lose its functionality by embedding the text file this can be outlined. The imperceptible modification is connected by this strategy. To identify hidden information to an eavesdropper's failure this proposed strategy strives for high security.

In 2012 in light of Huffman encoding for image stenography a novel method was proposed by RigDas and Themrichon Tuithung [14]. By adjusting the least significant bit (LSB) of each of the pixel's powers of cover image over the secret image/message before implanting and each piece of Huffman code of mystery Image/message is inserted inside the cover image the Huffman encoding is performed. The measure of the Huffman table and Huffman encoded bit stream are installed inside the image cover, to the beneficiary so that the stego-image moves toward becoming independent data.

In a spectrum (change) area of a digital medium (video, audio and image) the issue of separating indiscriminately data embedded over a wide band was considered by Li et al. [15] in 2013. In HOSTS by means of multicarrier spread-spectrum embedding to look for obscure data hidden we build up a novel multicarrier/signature iterative generalized least squares (M-IGLS) center strategy. Nor the embedding transporters neither the original host is accepted accessible.

3. Proposed methodology

3.1. Assumptions based steganography for motion vector

i.   In the event that the stego noise is encrypted or encoded before embedding to be independent of $V_{k,l}$ the stego noise $\eta_{k,l}$ is expected and of each other, which is a sensible supposition.

ii.   From the compressed video MV values directly acquired are locally optimal, which implies hiding information on MVs will move the local optimal MVs to non-optimal.

3.2. Based steganalysis MV value add-or-subtract-one

By steganography to break down the impact created on MVs the add-or-subtract-one (AOSO) operation is then exhibited, trailed by the extraction of new feature AoSo. The universal applicability of AoSo feature is broke down contrasted with existing highlights at long last.

Inter-MB coding generic structure is appeared in **Figure 4**. Inter-MB coding was presented by distortion that is spoken to by the contrast between recreated MB and current MB, and is principally because of truncation and quantization. With the Laplacian probability density function (PDF) since the dispersion of the 2D-DCT coefficients of PE can be roughly demonstrated as

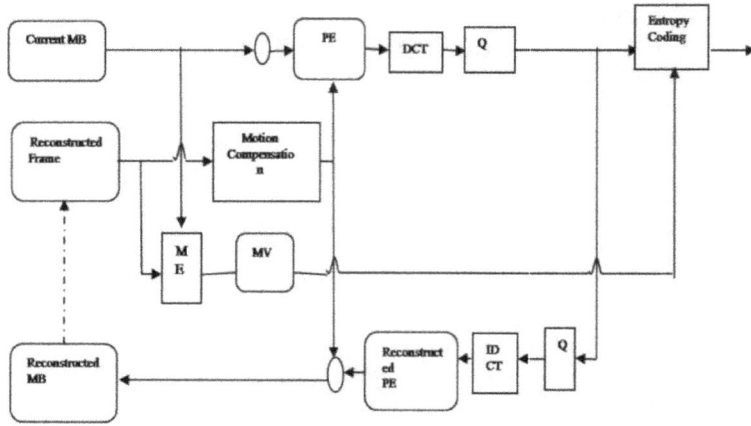

Figure 4. Inter-MB coding generic structure.

$$f_y(y) = \frac{\alpha \exp(-\alpha|y|)}{2} \qquad (4)$$

Where distribution of parameter is represented as α, with the accuracy of the motion estimation and it is mainly correlated. To get the coefficients y are then quantized

$$\tilde{y} = iQ, \quad if \ y \in \left[\left(i-\frac{1}{2}\right)Q, \left(i+\frac{1}{2}\right)Q\right] \qquad (5)$$

Where Q is the quantization step and i is an integer. The probability of the quantized coefficients can be calculated by

$$P_i = \int_{(i-\frac{1}{2})}^{(i+\frac{1}{2})} f_y(y)dy \qquad (6)$$

Thus the PDF of the residual signal introduced by quantization is

$$f_z(Z) = f_{|y-y|}(|y-y|) \qquad (7)$$

and

$$E[Z] = \frac{\tanh\left(\frac{\alpha Q}{4}\right)}{\alpha} \qquad (8)$$

E $[\varepsilon] \in (0, Q/4]$ is positively associated with Q, and is negatively correlated. To α and Q since the distortion of the coefficients DCT is connected, to α and Q likewise related the distortion of the SAD. The more genuine the distortion of the SAD might be is the bigger Q is and the littler α. At the point when motion estimation is much mistaken the worst case happen (e.g., the ME strategy is outlandish, the video content is FAST-moving and of complex texture) and with a large quantization step the DCT coefficients are compressed (e.g., the video bit rate of is set too little, or a huge incentive to a region around the quantization step is restricted).

4. Results and discussions

For lossy compressed images as quality estimation the PSNR is most usually utilized. The original image maximal power is the ratio of PSNR and twisted image noise power. In a wide unique range on the grounds that the powers of signals are for the most part, so it is spoken to in the logarithmic domain (**Figures 5–8**).

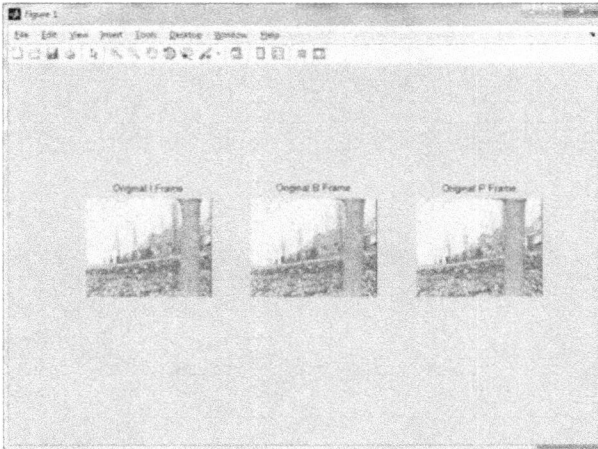

Figure 5. IBP frames chosen for embedding.

Figure 6. Motion vectors estimated.

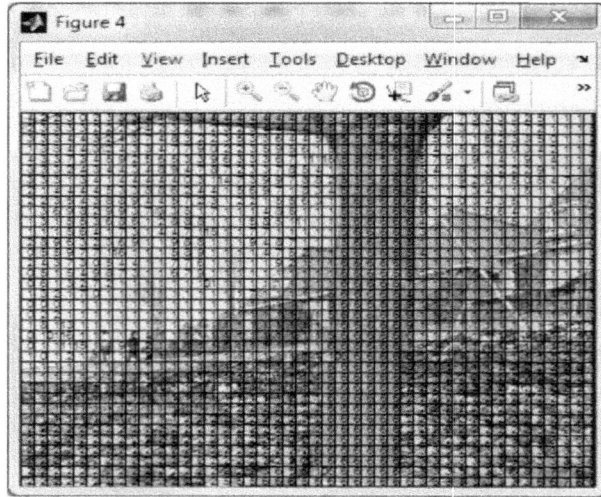

Figure 7. Macro block based processing.

Figure 8. Frame after embedding data.

The most significant difference between the error SSIM metrics and sensibility is the extraction of structural information. The luminance we see in a scene is the result of the illumination and the reflectance; however the structure of a protest is autonomous of the illumination. As the objective is to extricate the structural information from objects in an image, we wish to isolate the impact of the illumination. In other words, the structural information we consider should be independent of the luminance and the contrast.

In diagram X and Y are input signals to be measure. First, their luminance is compared. Second, the mean intensities are removed from each signal such that $\sum_{i=1}^{N} x_i = 0$ and $\sum_{i=1}^{N} y_i = 0$, and the signal contrast are estimated by the standard deviations. Third, each signal is normalized by dividing its standard deviation, so that the two signals being compared have both unit

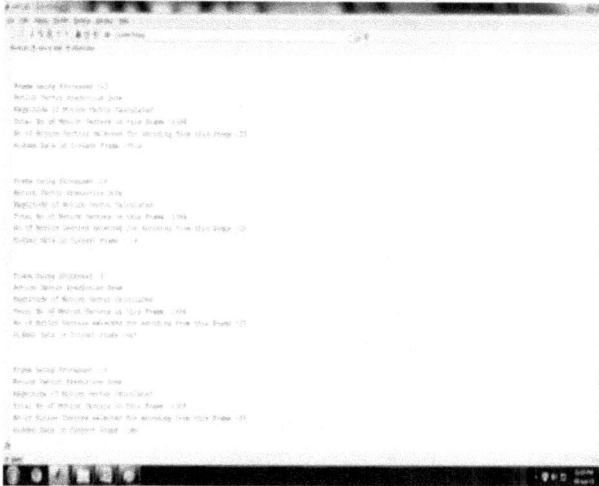

Figure 9. Data embedding process in frame by frame.

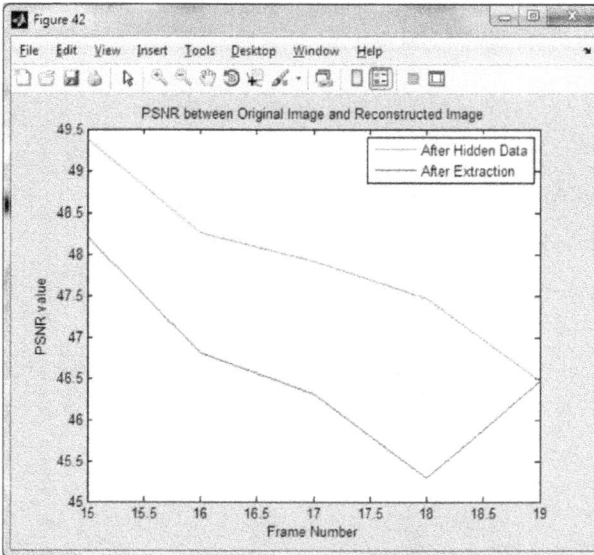

Figure 10. PSNR between original image and reconstructed image.

standard deviations. Next, the structure comparison is conducted on the two normalized signals. Finally, the three components: luminance, contrast, and structure comparison, are combined together to yield an overall similarity measure $S(X, Y)$. Here, the comparison functions should be defined such that $S(X, Y)$ can satisfy the three following conditions that should come to an image structure (**Figures 9** and **10**).

A.   Luminance Comparison

B.   Contrast Comparison

C.   Structure Comparison

5. Conclusion and future scope

This paper exhibited the ME method for searching the locally optimal MV value, and additionally the proof that MV construct steganography has slight impact based on SAD. To observe whether the actual MV is locally optimal, the operation of AoSo on MVs is employed and how deviates the actual SAD from the locally optimal one. For steganalysis the features based on AoSo activity are removed.

Analyzing the difference between the rated the motion value plays a crucial role that enables us to focus on difference between the locally optimal SAD and actual SAD after adding-or-subtracting-one operation on the motion value. Finally based on the motion vectors to perform the classification and extraction process two features sets are been used based on the fact that most motion vectors are locally optimal for most video codec's to complete this process. In the literature to conventional approaches announced the technique for proposed prevails to meet the requirement applications and detecting the steganalysis in videos compare.

Author details

Srinivas Bachu[1]* and Aravind Kumar Madam[2]

*Address all correspondence to: bachusrinivas@gmail.com

1 Department of Electronics and Communication Engineering, KL Deemed to be University, Hyderabad, Telangana, India

2 Department of Electronics and Communication Engineering, GVVIT, Bhimavaram, Andhra Pradesh, India

References

[1] Wang K, Zhao H, Wang H. Video steganalysis against motion vector-based steganography by adding or subtracting one motion vector value. IEEE Transactions on Information Forensics and Security. May 2014;**9**(5):741-751

[2] Srinivas B, Priyanka O. A novel approach for detection of motion vector-based video steganography by AOSO motion vector value. Proceedings of International Conference on Innovations in Computer Science & Engineering. Springer-AISC Series. **413**:225-233

[3] Kumar S, Biswas M. New method of noise removal in images using curvelet transform. In: International Conference on Computing, Communication & Automation (ICCCA), 15–16 May 2015, Noida, India

[4] Liu T-H, Chang L-W. An adaptive data hiding technique for binary images. In: 17th Proceedings of the International Conference on Pattern Recognition (ICPR) 2004. Cambridge, UK; 20 September 2004

[5] Wu HC, Wu NI, Tsai CS, Hwang MS. Image steganographic scheme based on pixel-value differencing and LSB replacement methods. IEE Proceedings–Vision Image and Signal Processing. 2005;**152**(5):611-615

[6] Carli M, Fariasy MCQ, Drelie Gelascaz E, Tedesco R, Neri A. Quality Assessment using Data Hiding on Perceptually Important. IEEE AREAS0-7803-9134-/05/$20.00©;2005

[7] Tseng H-W, Feng-Rong W, Hsieh C-P. Data hiding for binary images using weight mechanism. In: Proceedings of the Third International Conference on Intelligent Information Hiding and Multimedia Signal Processing (IIH-MSP 2007); Kaohsiung, Taiwan; Nov. 2007. pp. 26-28

[8] Mehboob B, Faruqui RA. A steganography implementation. In: International Symposium on Biometrics and Security Technologies. IEEE; 2008. pp. 1-5

[9] Medeni Mb O, El Mamoun S. A generalization of the PVD steganographic method. International Journal of Computer Science and Information Security. 2010;**8**(8):156-159

[10] Mahjabin T, Hossain SM, Haque MS. A block based data hiding method in images using pixel value differencing and LSB substitution method. IEEE; 2012

[11] Chaudhary A, Vasavada J, Raheja JL, Kumar S, Sharma M. A hash based approach for secure keyless steganography in lossless RGB images. In: 22nd International Conference on Computer Graphics and Vision; 2012

[12] Dasgupta K, Mandal JK, Dutta P. Hash based least significant bit technique for video steganography(Hlsb). International Journal of Security, Privacy and Trust Management (IJSPTM). April 2012;**1**(2)

[13] Chaudhary A, Vasavada JJ. A Hash Based Approach for Secure Keyless Image Steganography in Lossless RGB Images. IEEE; 2012

[14] Das R, Tuithung T. A Novel Steganography Method for Image Based on Huffman Encoding. IEEE; 2012

[15] Li M, Kulhandjian MK, Pados DA, Batalama SN, Medley MJ. Extracting spread-spectrum hidden data from digital media. IEEE Transactions on Information Forensics and Security. July 2013;**8**(7)

Chapter 5

Multilevel Steganography to Improve Secret Communication

Krishna Bhowal

Additional information is available at the end of the chapter

http://dx.doi.org/10.5772/intechopen.81599

Abstract

This chapter presents multilevel audio steganography, which describes a new model for hidden communication in secret communication technology. At least two embedding methods are used in such a way that the second method will use the first method as a carrier. The proposed method has several potential benefits in hidden communication. This method can be used to increase the level of security while transmitting the confidential information over public channels or internet and also can be used to provide two or more information hiding solutions simultaneously. The performance of the proposed method in terms of imperceptibility, capacity & security is measured through different experiments.

Keywords: audio steganography, multilevel steganography, secret communication, information security, imperceptibility, embedding capacity, discrete wavelet transform

1. Introduction

This chapter depicts multilevel audio steganography, which presents a new model for hidden communication. In multilevel steganography, at least two embedding methods are used in such a way that the second method may use the first method as a carrier. This approach has several potential benefits in hidden communication. It can be used to increase the level of security while transmitting the confidential information over public channels. It can also be used to provide two or more information hiding solutions simultaneously. Another important benefit is that the lower level embedding/extracting method and higher level embedding/extracting method are interrelated in terms of functionality and this makes the hidden communication harder to detect. If the cover object is interpreted by any adversary, only a decoy message or a partial message will be obtained.

The main aim of steganography is to hide secret information in digital cover. The alteration of the cover caused by embedding secret information remains invisible to the third party opponents. This is possible by designing an appropriate embedding algorithm and choosing a suitable cover. Therefore, there will be no significant dissimilarity between original cover and embedded cover. So, secret information not only is hidden inside the cover, but the fact of the secret information communication is also hidden. Each steganographic method may be characterized by following requirements. First, undetectability which is defined as the inability of detecting secret information inside the embedded cover. Actually, the distortion of the embedded cover convinces the opponent to analyze the statistical properties of the cover and compare them to the distinguishing properties of that cover. Therefore, imperceptibility or inaudibility is directly relational to the undetectability. Second, embedding capacity is defined as an amount of secret information which can be transmitted using a particular algorithm per unit of time. Third, steganographic cost, which defines the amount of alteration of the cover caused due to the secret information embedding method. The steganographic cost depends on the cover used as a carrier and also depends on embedding algorithm used.

For each steganographic method, there is always a trade-off between maximizing hiding capacity and remaining secret information undetected. Therefore, a certain level of tuning between embedding capacity and undetectability is required. If the embedding and extracting algorithm remains secret to the opponent, it can be used to transmit secret information freely. On the other hand, if the both algorithms are known to the opponent, anybody may be able to extract the secret information. This type of problem may be resolved by using the different encryption algorithms appropriate for a particular application. The encryption algorithm AES may be used to encrypt secret information before embedding it to the cover. Therefore, in this case, extracted information will not be readable by the opponent. There is a problem with this method, because the encryption key and the encrypted information are communicated using the same embedding technique. Thus, the encryption key and the secret information both will be revealed on successful detection. Alternatively, embedding capacity may be reduced due to embedding of the encryption key in cover object. The multilevel steganography was originally proposed by Al-Najjar for image steganography in [1]. The main idea in this paper was to hide a decoy image into LSB positions of the cover and the original secret information is embedded into the LSB positions of the decoy image.

Encryption and steganography are two general methods for hiding secret information [2–4]. Information is hidden using an encoding method that only authorized persons with the proper key can decode it in encryption. On the other hand, steganography hides secret information such a way that hidden information is imperceptible to the regular observer. The secret information can be embedded directly or some transformation can be applied to it before the embedding process. Generally, transformations include encryption, compression, transformation or a combination of digital transformation techniques. In [4], Vitaliev proposed two methods of information hiding. In the first method, plain text is hidden into an audio signal and in the second method; an audio file is hidden in an image object. In [5], Petitcolas et al. presented a method where a text object is hidden into another text object. In [6], Al-Najjar et al.

proposed a method where an audio file is embedded in an image after performing encryption and compression. In [7], Marvel proposed a hidden communication method by hiding of an image into another image in his Ph.D. Dissertation. In [8], Solanki presented a multimedia data hiding technique to hide an image into a video file in his Ph.D. Dissertation.

In [9], Lou et al. proposed an information hiding technique to protect a medical information. This paper suggests a multiple-layer data hiding technique in spatial domain. The reduced difference expansion method is utilized to embed the bit stream in the least significant bits (LSBs) of the expanded differences. A large amount of data is embedded in a medical image by using this method where quality of the image is also be maintained. Moreover, the original image can be restored after extracting the hidden data from the stego-image.

Cocktail party effect is used in audio steganography system where blind key concept is applied to resist the attack in the system [10]. Private key on the domain of cosine discrete transform (CDT) is used in steganographic algorithm in [11]. A new quantization technique is used in a steganographic method and the algorithm is designed based on DCT in [12]. A DNA structural concept is utilized in audio steganography in [13]. A novel audio steganography is designed using ZDT in [14]. Here encryption is done using indexed based chaotic sequence.

In this chapter, multilevel audio steganography is discussed to address the above stated problems. The proposed approach extends the concept of steganography to use it in more general purpose.

2. Improved secret communication using multilevel audio steganography

Multilevel steganography can be categorized as per the requirement of its application. Embedding capacity is the basic requirement in some of the applications where imperceptibility may be compromised in a certain level. On the other hand, imperceptibility is the main requirement in some of the applications where embedding capacity may be compromised in a certain level. So, the multilevel steganography may be classified as like below:

(i) Single message multiple covers—multilevel steganography denoted as **TYPE-I**

A message is embedded in multiple covers using several embedding functions to increase the level of security of the system. This approach provides better imperceptibility, but embedding capacity may be compromised in most of the cases.

(ii) Single cover multiple messages—multilevel steganography denoted as **TYPE-II**

Multiple messages are embedded in a single digital cover using several related embedding functions to increase the embedding capacity of the system. This approach provides better embedding capacity, but imperceptibility may be compromised in most of the cases.

2.1. Methodology

In this section, TYPE-I and TYPE-II types of multilevel steganography models are discussed [15].

2.1.1. Single message multiple covers—multilevel steganography model (TYPE-I)

Suppose, the Message is denoted as M, the Covers are denoted as C_i, the Intermediate Covers or stego-covers are denoted as I_i. Here, the value of i depends on the level of steganography, to be performed.

The message M is passed through the transformation T_i. The transformations may include compression, encryption or a transforms like Discrete Cosine Transform (DCT), Fourier Transform (FT) or Discrete Wavelet Transform (DWT), etc. Sometimes a combination of techniques may be used as required by the particular application.

Message embedding and extracting operations are performed by the embedding and extracting function pairs embed() and extract() and denoted by f and f′ respectively. The message embedding function may vary to improve the steganography attributes like imperceptibility, capacity, and robustness.

T_i = I means no transformation is applied. In the blind system, hidden information is extracted without using cover C_i at the receiving end.

The TYPE-I multilevel steganography model (for i = 3) is presented in **Figures 1** and **2**.

At the sender end, in phase 1, secret message M is embedded in cover object C_1 using transformation T_1 and embedding function f_1 and stego-object I_1 is generated. In the next phase, stego-object I_1 is hidden in another new cover object C_2 using transformation T_2 and

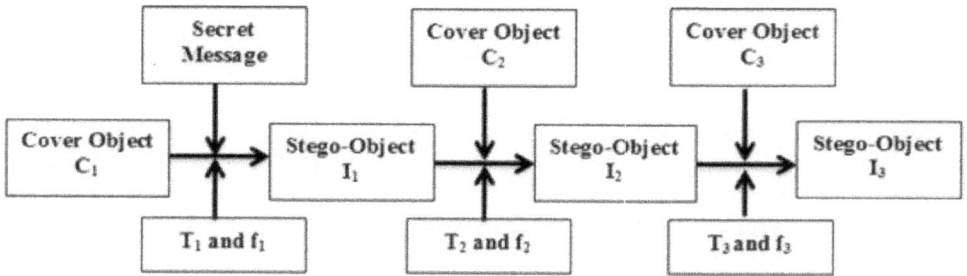

Figure 1. TYPE-I multilevel steganography model at the sender end for level = 3.

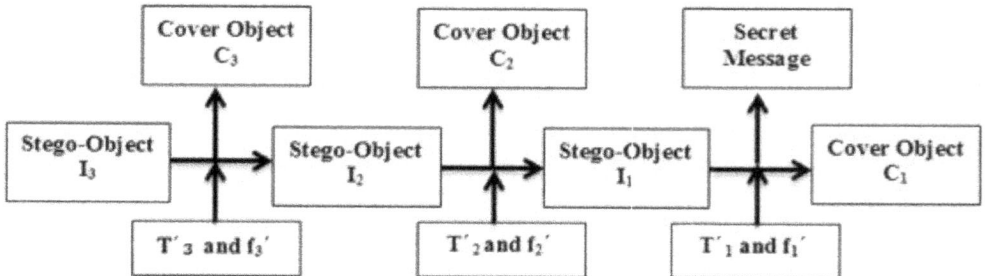

Figure 2. TYPE-I multilevel steganography model at the receiver end for level = 3.

embedding function f_2 and stego-object I_2 is generated. This process is continued as per the requirement of the application. There are three levels of embedding process is shown in **Figure 1**.

At the receiver end, according to the above 2 level embedding process, in phase 1, stego-object I_1 is generated from stego-object I_2 and applying T_2' transformation and f_2' embedding function. In the next phase, secret message M is generated from stego-object I_1 by applying T_1' transformation and f_1' embedding function. There are three level of extraction process shown in **Figure 2**.

Example of TYPE-I: 2 level steganography

Secret message embedding process:

Level-1: for i = 1

The cover is a grayscale image (C_1) and Message is a text message (M). Here, transmission T_1 is an encryption process, i.e., the secret message is encrypted using some standard encryption algorithm. The encrypted secret message bits are embedded at the 2nd LSB position of each pixel value of the cover image. The embedding function f_1 is defined as $f_1(mbit) = C_1.LSB(2)$ and f_1 is used to generate Intermediate cover or stego-cover I_1.

Leve-2: for i = 2

In this step, the cover is an audio signal (C_2) and Intermediate Cover or stego-cover is I_1. I_1 is generated in the previous step and it is an embedded image. The image is converted to a bit stream and each bit is embedded at the 1st LSB position of each audio sample of the audio signal. Here, transformation $T_2 = I$ and the embedding function f_2 is defined as $f_2(ibit) = C_2.LSB(1)$ and f_2 is used to generate intermediate cover or stego-cover I_2.

Secret message extraction process:

Level-2: for i = 2

The Intermediate Cover (I_2) is an embedded audio signal and the embedded image bits are extracted from the 1st LSB position of each audio sample. Here, transformation $T_2' = I$ and the extracting function f_2' is defined as $f_2'(ibit) = I_2.LSB(1)$ and f_2' is used to generate intermediate cover or stego-cover I_1.

Level-1: for i = 1

The Intermediate Cover (I_1) is an embedded image and the message bits are extracted from the 2nd LSB position of each pixel value of the embedded image. Here, transmission T_1' is a decryption process of the corresponding encryption algorithm used during embedding process. The extraction function f_1' is defined as $f_1'(mbit) = I_1.LSB(2)$ and f_1' is used to generate secret message M.

2.1.2. Single cover multiple messages—multilevel steganography model (TYPE-II)

Suppose, the Cover is denoted as C, the Messages are denoted as M_i, the Intermediate Covers or stego-covers are denoted as I_i. Here, the value of i depends on the level of steganography, to be performed.

The messages M_i are passed through the transformation T_i like previous section. The TYPE-II multilevel steganography model (for $i = 3$) is presented in **Figures 3** and **4**. At the sender end, in phase 1, secret message M_1 is embedded in a cover object C using transformation T_1 and embedding function f_1 and stego-object I_1 is generated. In the next phase, another message M_2 is hidden in stego-object I_1 using transformation T_2 and embedding function f_2 and stego-object I_2 is generated. This process is continued as per the requirement of the application. There are three level of embedding process as shown in **Figure 3**.

At the receiver end, according to the above 2 level embedding process, in phase 1, message M_2 is generated from stego-object I_2 by applying T_2' transformation and f_2' embedding function. In the next phase, secret message M_1 is generated from stego-object I_1 by applying T_1' transformation and f_1' embedding function. There are three level of extraction process shown in **Figure 4**.

Example of TYPE-II: 2 level steganography

Secret message embedding process:

Level-1: for i = 1

The cover is an audio clip (C) and the two secret messages are M_1 and M_2. Here, transmission T_1 is Discrete Wavelet Transform (DWT) and Inverse DWT (IDWT) of the audio signal. The M_1 message bits are embedded at the 2nd LSB position of each DWT coefficient of the audio signal. The embedding function f_1 is defined as $f_1(mbit) = C.LSB(2)$ and f_1 and IDWT are used to generate Intermediate cover or stego-cover I_1.

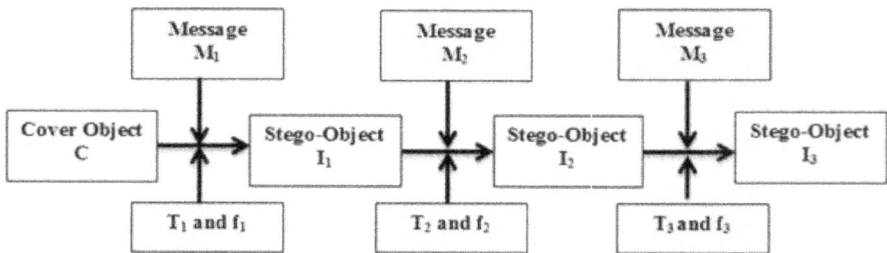

Figure 3. TYPE-II multilevel steganography model at the sender end for level = 3.

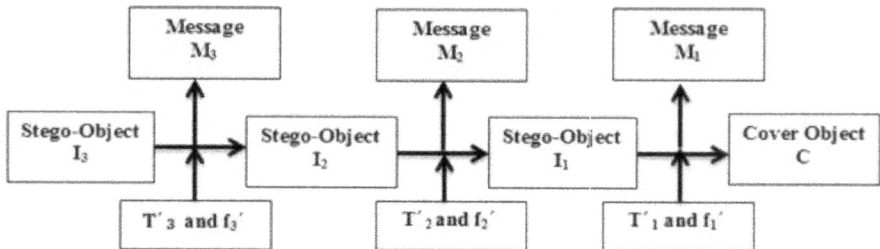

Figure 4. TYPE-II multilevel steganography model at the receiver end for level = 3.

Level-2: for i = 2

In this step, the cover is an Intermediate Cover or stego-cover (I_1). I_1 is generated in the previous step and it is an embedded audio signal. The M_2 message bits are embedded at the 1st LSB position of each audio sample of the audio signal. Here, transformation $T_2 = I$ and the embedding function f_2 is defined as $f_2(mbit) = C.LSB(1)$ and f_2 is used to generate Intermediate cover or stego-cover I_2.

Secret message extracting process:

Level-2: for i = 2

The Intermediate Cover (I_2) is an embedded audio signal and the M_2 message bits are extracted from the 1st LSB position of each audio sample. Here, transformation $T_2' = I$ and the extracting function f_2' is defined as $f_2'(abit) = I_2.LSB(1)$ and f_2' is used to generate Intermediate cover or stego-cover I_1.

Level-1: for i = 1

The Intermediate Cover (I_1) is an embedded audio and the message bits are extracted from the 2nd LSB position of each DWT coefficient of the embedded audio signal. Here, transmission T_1' is DWT and IDWT of the embedded audio signal. The extraction function f_1' is defined as $f_1'(abit) = I_1.LSB(2)$ and f_1' is used to generate secret message M_1.

3. Experimental result and discussion

Proposed algorithm has been tested on 10 audio sequences from different music styles (classic, jazz, country, pop, rock, etc.). All the Clips are 44.1 kHz sampled mono audio files, represented by 16 bits per sample, and length of the clips ranges from 10 to 20 seconds. An image and the all audio clips are used to test TYPE-I type of algorithm and all the audio clips are used to test TYPE-II algorithm.

3.1. Imperceptibility test

Basic requirement is the imperceptibility in most of the applications, i.e., after hiding secret messages in audio signals; the quality of the embedded audio signals should remain same as original audio signals. Here, Subjective Difference Grade (SDG), Objective Difference Grade (ODG) and Signal-to-Noise Ratio (SNR) is used to measure the imperceptibility of the proposed method. The SDG and ODG listening tests use the 5-grade scale shown in **Table 1**.

3.1.1. Objective quality measurements

The ODG measurements of different audio clips are provided using the advanced ITU-R BS.1387 standard [16] and are calculated using the Opera software [17] which is implemented by maintaining ITU-R BS.1387 standard. ODG values for TYPE-I and TYPE-II approaches are reported in **Tables 2** and **3** and respectively for different types of audio signals. The ODG

Audio standard	Subjective difference grade (SDG)	Objective difference grade (ODG)
Indistinguishable	5	0.0
Distinguishable, but not aggravating	4	−1.0
Slightly aggravating	3	−2.0
Aggravating	2	−3.0
Very aggravating	1	−4.0

Table 1. Subjective and objective grades for audio quality measurement.

Audio types	Objective difference grade (ODG)	Subjective difference grade (SDG)	Signal-to-noise ratio (SNR (dB))
A1	−0.51	5.0	92.25
A2	−0.63	4.9	91.41
A3	−0.61	4.9	91.63
A4	−0.52	5.0	92.43
A5	−0.49	5.0	92.54
A6	−0.50	5.0	92.35
A7	−0.64	4.9	91.55
A8	−0.59	4.9	91.57
A9	−0.49	5.0	92.36
A10	−0.53	4.9	91.78

Table 2. ODG, SDG & SNR values for different audio clips (TYPE-I, level = 2).

Audio types	Objective difference grade (ODG)	Subjective difference grade (SDG)	Signal-to-noise ratio (SNR (dB))
A1	−0.61	4.9	90.15
A2	−0.72	4.8	89.31
A3	−0.70	4.8	88.93
A4	−0.61	4.9	90.41
A5	−0.59	4.9	90.22
A6	−0.60	4.9	90.16
A7	−0.68	4.8	89.25
A8	−0.69	4.8	89.36
A9	−0.58	4.9	90.19
A10	−0.63	4.8	89.14

Table 3. ODG, SDG & SNR values for different audio clips (TYPE-II, level = 2).

values for TYPE-I model are −0.49 to −0.64 and the ODG values for TYPE-II model are −0.58 to −0.72.

3.1.2. Subjective quality evaluation

Subjective quality measurements [18, 19] have been performed to evaluate the imperceptibility of our proposed data hiding scheme. The output of the subjective tests is an average of the quality ratings called a Mean Opinion Score (MOS). SDG values for TYPE-I and TYPE-II approaches are reported in **Tables 2** and **3** respectively for different types of audio signals. The SDG values for TYPE-I model are 4.9–5.0 and the SDG values for TYPE-II model are 4.8–4.9.

3.1.3. Signal-to-noise ratio (SNR) measurement

The signal-to-noise ratio (SNR) value is used to make the difference between the original and embedded audio signal [20]. Normally, if the SNR value is higher than 50 dB, then the secret data which are hidden in the audio signal are imperceptible to the human auditory system. The SNR values for TYPE-I and TYPE-II approaches are measured using equation no. (1) and are reported in **Tables 2** and **3** respectively for different types of audio signals.

$$\text{SNR} = 10 \, \log_{10} \frac{\sum_{i=1}^{N} x^2(i)}{\sum_{i=1}^{N} \left(x(i) - y(i)\right)^2} \tag{1}$$

The ODG, SDG, and SNR values are evaluated for different audio signals. Here, 2 level multilevel steganography is performed for TYPE-I and TYPE-II models. The results are presented in **Tables 2** and **3** of TYPE-I and TYPE-II models respectively. For simplicity, 10 audio clips are denoted as A1, A2, A3, A4, A5, A6, A7, A8, A9 and A10.

3.2. Embedding capacity analysis

One of the basic requirements of the secret communication using steganography is increasing the embedding capacity by keeping the imperceptibility in a desired level. In the proposed system, if TYPE-I approach is followed, embedding capacity is not so much desired level, because imperceptibility given higher priority. But, if TYPE-II approach is followed, multiple messages may be embedded in a single cover object by designing appropriate transforms and embedding functions.

The embedding capacity is measured by the number of bits that can be hidden into the audio signal per unit of time. Suppose, D is the duration of the original audio clip in seconds and B is the number of secret information bits. Now, the capacity is measured as:

$$\text{Capacity} = B/D \text{ bps} \tag{2}$$

In this work, the frequency of the carrier signal is fixed, i.e., 44.1 Kz is considered. The sample rate 44.1 kHz means 44,100 samples per second in one channel.

3.3. Security analysis

Security is another very important requirement of hidden communication using steganography. A data hiding method is said to be secured if an adversary would not be able to detect or modify or remove the hidden information in the embedded object. To measure the security of the proposed technique, following scenarios may be considered:

a.   The adversary has no information about the hidden information in the host object. So, the proposed method is secure.

b.   The adversary has no idea about the embedding or extracting algorithm. Therefore, the proposed method is secure.

c.   The adversary has information only about the embedding and extracting algorithm. In this case, the adversary cannot precede the extraction operation without knowing the actual location is used to hide information.

By minimizing the bit flipping during the embedding process is normally guaranteed that the algorithm designed to estimate the hidden data based on statistical analysis may be effectively disabled.

In TYPE-I approach, a message is hidden in a cover object and that stego-cover object is hidden in another cover object, and so on. This approach increases the level of security of the system. Again, the number of levels is used during the embedding process in multilevel steganography is very important information at the receiving end. That means, security may be increased by varying the number of levels during embedding process. Along with this, any of the encryption algorithms may be used at a transformation phase of the system to increase the security of the system.

3.4. Comparative study

In this section, a comparative study is performed with the very recent works on audio steganography as well as audio watermarking proposed by different authors. Actually, impartial comparison is very difficult, because every approach have its own characteristics and also designed to fulfill certain basic requirement. Anyway, most of the algorithm has some common characteristics like embedding capacity, imperceptibility etc. Here, comparisons are performed based on embedding capacity and imperceptibility (SNR & ODG) of the system and reported in **Table 4**.

The method in [21] provides a significant performance in the different properties of the data embedding technique. The method offers moderate data hiding capacity solutions for data hiding in audio file even though the imperceptibility in terms of SNR and ODG is below average in some of the issues. The important achievement of this scheme is robustness against different attacks such as echo, filtering, and noise added. The method in [23] achieves a low embedding capacity for the three audio files considered. The imperceptibility in terms of SNR is below average, but the imperceptibility (ODG) is moderate in this scheme. This scheme has a good performance against compression and the maximum of BER against this is about 1%. The

Algorithm	Capacity (bps)	SNR (dB)	ODG
Xiang et al. [21]	2	42.8–44.4	$-1.66 < ODG < -1.88$
Mansour et al. [22]	4.3	29.5	Not reported
Fallahpour et al. [23]	3 k	30.55	-0.6
Fallahpour et al. [24]	2–6 k	Not reported	$-0.6 < ODG < -1.7$
Fallahpour et al. [25]	11 k	30	-0.7
Kang et al. [26]	64	30–45	$-1 < ODG$
Nishimura et al. [27]	8	Not reported	$-3 < ODG < -1$
Proposed	44,100	92.54	$-0.49 < ODG < -0.64$

Table 4. Comparative studies among different works.

algorithms in [24, 25] offer low embedding capacity, good transparency, and reasonably robustness against selected attacks. The scheme in [24] provides very a low data hiding rate, high distortion, and very robust scheme, while that in [25] provides very low embedding capacity, highly distorted signals (SNR is 30 dB), and moderate robustness against some attacks.

The most important achievement of the proposed method is better imperceptibility in terms of SNR and ODG with higher embedding capacity. The comparison presented in **Table 4** demonstrates the superiority in both capacity and imperceptibility of the proposed method with respect to the schemes discussed in the literature. The proposed method can hide much more information by introducing less distortion in the audio file. In brief, the proposed method achieves higher embedding capacity if we compare it to methods with similar imperceptibility.

The data presented in **Table 4** confirms that the proposed method have better performance in terms of embedding capacity and imperceptibility.

4. Conclusion

In this chapter, two multilevel steganography models are proposed. Normally, the requirement of data hiding application varies from application to application. The proposed models are designed such a way that the customization may be done as per the requirement of a particular application. That means, number of embedding and extracting levels, number of messages to be hidden, and number of cover objects to be used etc. are customizable. The suggested model enhances the security level of the steganography technique in terms of imperceptibility as well as capacity. The stego-object, usually does not seem suspicious, since it looks similar to the original object to the general observer. An adversary may be satisfied with the decoy as the hidden message and may not use additional tools to look further. The authorized receivers have information about the hidden message, as well as the information required to extract the message. Hence, it can be concluded that the proposed models enhanced potentially more security to information hiding.

Acknowledgements

First and most of all, I thank God, the almighty for giving me this opportunity and granting me the ability to carry on the process successfully.

I take this opportunity to show my gratitude to all my teachers, starting from my school days to this day, who have guided me throughout my pursuit for knowledge, who have given me the opportunity to express my thoughts, who gave patient listening to my ideas even though many a time it was unreasonable. This book chapter looks like in its current form due to the guidance and support of several people. I am especially grateful to my supervisor Dr. Debasree Chanda (Sarkar), for her warm encouragement, critical comments, and thoughtful guidance. I also owe thanks to Dr. Partha Pratim Sarkar, Professor, for his insightful discussion, offering valuable advice, encouraging comments, and suggestions throughout this work. Despite his extremely busy schedule, he has gone through the thesis in depth.

Lastly but not the least, I acknowledge the Academy of Technology, Hooghly, Kolkata, India.

Conflict of interest

Replace the entirety of this text with the 'conflict of interest' declaration.

Author details

Krishna Bhowal

Address all correspondence to: ykbhowal@yahoo.co.in

Department of MCA, Academy of Technology, Kolkata, India

References

[1] Al-Najjar J. The decoy: Multi-level digital multimedia steganography model. In: Proc. of 12th WSEAS International Conference on Communications, Heraklion, Greece, July. 2008. pp. 23-25

[2] Anderson RJ, Petitcolas FAP. On the limits of the steganography. IEEE Journal of Selected Areas in Communications. 1998;**16**(4):474-481

[3] Artz D. Digital steganography: Hiding data within data. IEEE Internet Computing Archive. 2001;**5**(3):75-80

[4] Vitaliev D. Digital Security and Privacy for Human Rights Defenders. Dublin: The International Foundation for Human Right Defenders; 2007. pp. 77-81

[5] Petitcolas FAP, Anderson RJ, Kuhn MG. Information hiding–A survey. Proceedings of the IEEE, Special Issue on Protection of Multimedia Content. 1999;**87**:1062-1078

[6] Al-Najjar AJ, Alvi AK, Idrees SU, Al-Manea AM. Hiding Encrypted Speech Using Stega-nography. China, Sept. 15–17: WSEAS Beijing; 2007. pp. 275-281

[7] Marvel LM. Image steganography for hidden communication", Ph.D. Dissertation. Uni-versity of Delaware, spring; 1999

[8] Solanki M. Multimedia Data Hiding: From Fundamental Issues to Practical Techniques", Ph.D. Dissertation. Santa Barbara, US: University of California; 2005

[9] Lou DC, Hu MC, Liu JL. Multiple layer data hiding scheme for medical images. Computer Standards and Interfaces. 2009;**31**(2):329-335

[10] Gupta Banik B, Bandyopadhyay SK. Blind key based attack resistant audio steganography using cocktail party effect. Security and Communication Networks. 2018;**2018**(1781384): 1-21

[11] Lorente AS, Cumbrera R, Fonseca Y. Steganographic algorithm of private key on the domain of the cosine discrete transform. Revista Cubana de Ciencias Informáticas. 2016; **10**(2):116-131

[12] Amin M, Abdullkader HM, Ibrahem HM, Sakr AS. A steganographic method based on DCT and new quantization technique. International Journal of Network Security. 2014; **16**(4):265-270

[13] Tank RM, Vasava HD, Agrawal V. DNA-based audio steganography. Oriental Journal of Computer Science and Technology. 2015;**8**(1):43-48

[14] Sharma S, Yadav VK, Trivedi MC, Gupta A. Audio steganography using ZDT: Encryption using indexed based chaotic sequence. In: ICTCS '16 Proceedings of the Second Interna-tional Conference on Information and Communication Technology for Competitive Strat-egies, Article No. 66 , Udaipur, India — March 04–05, 2016

[15] Bhowal K, Chanda(Sarkar) D, Biswas S, Sarkar PP. Enhanced secret communication using multilevel audio steganography. International Journal of Computational Engineering Research. 2016;**6**(10):6-12

[16] Thiede T, Treurniet WC, Bitto R, Schmidmer C, Sporer T, Beerens JG, et al. PEAQ–The ITU standard for objective measurement of perceived audio quality. Journal of the Audio Engineering Society. 2000;**48**(1/2):3-29

[17] OPTICOM OPERA software site, [Online]. Available: http://www.opticom.de/products/ opera.html

[18] Unoki M, Imabeppu K, Hamada D, Haniu A, Miyauchi R. Embedding limitations with digital-audio watermarking method based on cochlear delay characteristics. Journal of Information Hiding and Multimedia Signal Processing. 2011;**2**(1):1-23

[19] Wang S, Unoki M. Speech watermarking method based on formant tuning. IEICE Transactions on Information and Systems. 2015;**E98-D**(1):29-37

[20] Quackenbush SR, Barnwell IIITP, Clements MA. Objective Measures of Speech Quality. Englewood Cliffs: Prentice Hall; 1988

[21] Xiang S, Kim JH, Huang J. Audio watermarking robust against time-scale modification and MP3 compression. Signal Processing. 2008;**88**(10):2372-2387

[22] Mansour M, Tewfik A. Data embedding in audio using time-scale modification. IEEE Transactions on Speech and Audio Processing. 2005;**13**(3):432-440

[23] Fallahpour M, Megías D. High capacity audio watermarking using fft amplitude interpolation. IEICE Electronics Express. 2009;**6**:1057-1063

[24] Fallahpour M, Megías D. High capacity method for real-time audio data hiding using the fft transform. In: Advances in Information Security and its Application. Berlin, Germany: Springer-Verlag; 2009. pp. 91-97

[25] Fallahpour M, Megías D. High capacity audio watermarking using the high frequency band of the wavelet domain. In: Multimedia Tools and Applications. Vol. 52. New York, NY, USA: Springer; 2011. pp. 485-498

[26] Kang X, Yang R, Huang J. Geometric invariant audio watermarking based on an LCM feature. IEEE Transactions on Multimedia. 2011;**13**:181-190

[27] Nishimura A. Audio data hiding that is robust with respect to aerial transmission and speech codecs. International Journal of Innovative Computing, Information and Control. 2010;**6**:1389-1400

www.ingramcontent.com/pod-product-compliance
Lightning Source LLC
Chambersburg PA
CBHW081240190326
41458CB00016B/5858